Life Streams

Life Streams

A lyfe[B] resource for spiritual growth

Adapted from Renovaré's bestselling
A Spiritual Formation Workbook

James Bryan Smith with Lynda L. Graybeal

BIBLE
SOCIETY

ISBN 978-0-564-04726-0

This edition published in 2010 by Bible Society Resources Ltd

Typeset in 10/14pt ITC Quay Sans by Bible Society Resources Ltd
Design by Chris Gander Design Associates
Printed in the UK

Bible Society Resources Ltd
Stonehill Green, Westlea,
Swindon SN5 7DG

Visit **bibleresources.org.uk** and **renovare.info**

Contents

Foreword

For some time I participated in two Spiritual Formation Groups simultaneously and was immeasurably enriched by both experiences. The first group was composed of only myself and one other person, the author of this book. The second included myself and three other individuals.

In the fall of 1988, Jim Smith and I started meeting just to see how a nurturing fellowship of mutual accountability might work. I cannot tell you how encouraging and fun-filled those first meetings were: we laughed at our foibles and rejoiced in our successes; we prayed; we made confession; we brought the grace of forgiveness; we made mutual covenants; we challenged and encouraged each other. They were high, holy, hilarious times.

In time, Jim and I were led to study many small group movements such as the Benedictines in the fourth century, the Franciscans in the thirteenth century, the Methodists in the eighteenth century, and Alcoholics Anonymous in the twentieth century. We also began developing a balanced vision of Christian faith and practice and a practical strategy for spiritual growth and much more. The second group came a bit later, and now a third has developed, but each has been equally encouraging. Why do I continue to be in Spiritual Formation groups? Briefly, let me explain why they mean so much to me.

First, I like the sense of community. None of us is supposed to live the Christian life alone. We gain strength and help from others.

Second, I like the nurturing character. The rule for our weekly gatherings is a good one: give encouragement as often as possible; advice, once in a great while; reproof, only when absolutely necessary; and judgement, never.

Third, I like the intentionality. Our purpose is to become better disciples of Jesus Christ. Everything is orientated around this single goal.

Fourth, I like the loving accountability. I need others to ask hard questions about my prayer experiences, temptations and struggles, and plans for spiritual growth.

Fifth, I like the balanced vision. To be baptised into the great streams of Christian faith and practice helps to free me from my many provincialisms.

Sixth, I like the practical strategy. I want and need realistic handles that actually move me forward into Christlikeness.

Seventh, I like the freedom and the fun. These groups encourage discipline without rigidity, accountability without manipulation.

I enthusiastically recommend this workbook to you. It's a more concise version published in the UK, based on the original US edition first released in the 1990s. It is the fruit of extensive study and research into group dynamics and the nature of spiritual development. It also has the ambience of those early meetings Jim and I had together. And though I have moved some distance from Jim and we are no longer able to meet together, I still remember well those times of high, holy hilarity!

Richard J. Foster

Preface

Life Streams is the result of a remarkable relationship between two unique organisations.

Renovaré (pronounced Ren-o-var-ey) was founded by Richard Foster in 1988. It offers a balanced vision and a practical strategy for spiritual growth. James Bryan Smith and Lynda Graybeal wrote *A Spiritual Formation Workbook* to help small groups make this vision a reality and thousands of people are now in Renovaré groups around the world.

Lyfe is an initiative of Bible Society, known internationally as British and Foreign Bible Society, founded over 200 years ago. Lyfe is a breakthrough in experiencing God through the Bible in a café, bar or some other public space. It takes seriously the idea that where we encounter God in Scripture is a big influence on what we receive from him.

Renovaré's *A Spiritual Formation Workbook* with Bible Society's lyfe project is an explosive mix of historic orthodox Christian faith and a new way of connecting God, life and us. By doing all this in a public setting, the experience is more intense and more meaningful.

It all started when Richard Foster first stepped into my office back in 1994. I was a lowly editor at his publishing house, but the conversation we had changed my life. Now I not only lead the work of Bible Society but also serve on the board of Renovaré.

The challenge that Richard put in front of me all those years ago was not to see how far apart I could keep God and daily life, but how integrated they could become. Later I developed the original lyfe project as an attempt to connect the Bible to the kind of life that I was experiencing myself. Through *Life Streams* I pray that you too will encounter the God of the Bible as you try to see how far you can fold your life into his.

James Catford
Group Chief Executive, Bible Society and Chair of Renovaré Britain & Ireland

Introduction

WHAT IS RENOVARÉ?

Renovaré (a Latin word meaning 'to renew') exists to inspire and support individuals in developing integrated and fulfilled lives as disciples of Jesus Christ. Christian in commitment, international in scope, and cross-denominational in breadth, it was founded as an initiative working for the renewal of the Church of Jesus Christ in all her multifaceted expressions. Its focus is the local church.

Although begun in the United States, the expressions of Renovaré around the world are led locally with full autonomy to develop within their own cultural contexts. In Britain and Ireland, the first Chair was James Catford, Group Chief Executive of Bible Society. *Life Streams* is more concise than the original US version of *A Spiritual Formation Workbook* and reflects the different ways in which people learn and receive their education around the world. The Renovaré website can be entered directly at www.renovare.info or via the US site www.renovare.us, where news updates, pastoral letters, teaching, recommended resources and information on events are available.

How does Renovaré encourage growth in faith and character?

God is inviting us to go on a journey into his heart and into the good life made available through Jesus; 'I came that they may have life, and have it abundantly' (John 10.10). But entering into this abundant life takes more than wishful thinking; it takes a well-thought-out, feasible plan. Renovaré exists to put such a plan in place.

The secret of this approach is the combination of three very important ingredients. The first is *balance*. To be spiritually healthy, we need balance in our spiritual lives, just as physical health needs a balance in diet and exercise. Renovaré is founded upon the six major areas of discipline found in the life of Christ and the corresponding Six Traditions seen in the history of the Church. Renovaré emphasises balance.

The second ingredient is *knowledge*. Many of us do not become Jesus' disciples for one reason: we lack information about the spiritual disciplines. We dream about being true followers, imagine ourselves being committed disciples, but how do we actually do it? What steps do we take? What activities do we engage in that will help us grow closer to God? It is as if we are looking across a great chasm, longing for the other side, discontent with where we are, yet unable to cross the bridge because we do not know how to start. The Renovaré approach provides that knowledge: what to do and how to do it.

The third ingredient is mutual *encouragement and accountability*. Once we find a balanced plan and a knowledge of how to use it, the only thing left for us is to do it. Unfortunately, for most of us this is the hardest part. Ingrained habits hamper us from changing the way we are. The secret to breaking these ingrained habits is the strength found in joining forces with others who have a similar mission. They provide the encouragement we need to start across the chasm and the accountability we need to keep us on the bridge. Renovaré's strategy utilises the God-given strength we gain from each other.

How a Spiritual Formation Group works

A Spiritual Formation Group helps you put yourself in a place where God can transform your life from the inside out. We learn how we can practise the spiritual disciplines, and how to encourage one another in our individual spiritual growth through reflection, discussion, mutual support and prayer. There are some exercises to do at home to deepen our understanding.

There are several advantages of this kind of group:

- It is *intentional*: the single goal is for those involved to become better disciples of Jesus Christ, through practising the spiritual disciplines and encouraging one another.

- It is *small*, comprising between two and seven people.

- There is a sense of *community*: none of us is supposed to live the Christian life alone.

- It is *accountable*: we benefit from having others alongside us as we face spiritual challenges.

A Spiritual Formation Group is not a prayer group, though it incorporates prayer. It is not a support group, though support is found there. And it is not a Bible study, though the Bible is used by the group. It is a group that focuses on what God has done, is doing, and will do in our lives.

Overall, Spiritual Formation Groups answer the question: *What will help me grow spiritually?* while each gathering of a Spiritual Formation Group focuses on two issues: *What has God been doing in my life? What do I plan to do before the next meeting to make space for him to do even more?*

What's involved

A Renovaré Spiritual Formation Group is realistic and practical – and fun. The fruit of extensive study and research into group dynamics and the nature of spiritual development, it is designed to draw people closer to God and to each other. From two to six (or maximum seven) people gather regularly to study, to share their past experiences, and to make plans for the week ahead. This is done easily by following a suggested 'Order of Meeting.'

At this stage, you are seeking to find one to five other people who are willing to gather for nine weeks to test-drive this strategy. There is no one leader of these meetings and everyone who participates shares this facilitating role – which is not difficult. The choice of who will guide the group each week is best made in advance, perhaps at the end of the previous meeting.

During each gathering (which should last between sixty and ninety minutes) that week's leader guides the group through a series of opening words, a question-and-answer session, and a closing time of prayer. Within this flexible format, members are reminded of their task, enabled to hear from one another, share, plan, and dream with each other. It is within this framework that the balance, the knowledge, and the encouragement and accountability are nurtured.

A word of encouragement

If you decide that you would like to form a Spiritual Formation Group, read through several of the sessions on your own. These can be used by individuals as a personal study but, just as it takes 'two to tango', so also it takes at least two to covenant. That is, the sessions will work best when done in the context of a group of two or more where the members can share and plan and lovingly hold one another accountable.

If you have decided to try this strategy, please keep in mind that we at Renovaré have no desire to control your actions or to demand that you use it exactly as it has been designed. We are committed to the Church, and this plan is our gift to the Church.

Also, we are not concerned that you use the Renovaré name for your group or groups within your church; some simply use the name 'Formation Group'. For you to grow closer to God and to your Christian sisters and brothers is our heart's desire. We cheerfully offer you and your church this theologically sound and experientially effective small-group strategy which comes from doing research for several years, listening to God, and responding to the needs of people. May God bless you richly in this endeavour.

How to use this Workbook

The plan itself is very simple. However, you must take a few steps to get a Spiritual Formation Group started. First find a partner or partners and learn about the basic approach. Forming a group is discussed in the next section of this workbook.

At least one, or maybe all Spiritual Formation Group members, lack the first two ingredients necessary for spiritual growth: *balance* and *knowledge*. This workbook contains eight sessions that will provide these two ingredients.

- **Session One** (see p.23) provides the 'big picture' that is our model, Jesus Christ, and also our illustration, the Six Traditions of the Church.

- **Sessions Two to Seven** (see pp.31–72) provide a basic understanding of six areas of discipline that make up this balanced diet along with an explanation of how they function in our lives.

- **Session Eight** (see. p.73) brings it all together providing you with the tools you will need to do a regular group in the future – if your group chooses to do so.

- We encourage you to meet one more time (Session Nine), using the **Order of Meeting** (see p.79), to give the regular group meeting a try.

Within each session look for the Group Discussion boxes for subjects to be debated within the group. There is also a range of exercises designed for individual or group study. When you reach each of the exercises the Workbook will make clear whether they should be undertaken within the group or away from the meeting. Those exercises done away from the meeting should be discussed at the next group meeting.

Once you have given the group meeting a try, decide whether or not to continue meeting. After the group has gone through the nine-week trial period, it will have:

- a functional knowledge of the Six Traditions

- a knowledge of how they are woven into our daily lives

- practical experience in each area

- a sense of how working as a group enhances our ability to accomplish our goals.

At this point the Spiritual Formation Group will need to decide its future by working through the **Evaluation** (see p.85) and the series of questions, designed to help the group plan for its future.

We have found it best for those who are willing to continue meeting to make a six-month commitment to stay with the Renovaré approach. At the end of the six months, the group can re-evaluate themselves once again, using the **Evaluation** chapter. Should any member or members of the group decide to stop here, or should the entire group decide to disband, the evaluation and planning section provides a graceful way to leave or break up. No group or individual should feel pressure to continue in a plan that does not meet their needs. We realise that it will not fit everyone. Even groups that meet over many years need to remember the importance of periodic evaluation.

Starting a Group

'Our existing churches and denominations do not have active, well-designed, intently pursued plans to accomplish [fulfilling the Great Commission] in their members ... you will not find any widely influential element of our church leadership that has a plan – not a vague wish or dream, but a plan for implementing all phases of the Great Commission,'

Dallas Willard, *The Spirit of the Disciplines* p.167

The strategy offered through the Spiritual Formation Groups is the sort of plan called for by Dallas Willard in the quotation above. In drawing people closer to God and deepening their spiritual lives, it contributes to the fulfilment of the Great Commission, Jesus' command to 'make disciples' (Matthew 28.19b).

Whether you want to go deeper with God, or are longing to see Jesus' command fulfilled, this strategy will help you take steps towards your goal.

This chapter sets outs the preliminaries for anyone who would like to start a Spiritual Formation Group. If you are still wondering whether this is the right step for you, this chapter will fill in some of the gaps. If you are already motivated, it will give you pointers about how to get going.

Working with an existing group

You may already be meeting in a small group, whether as part of a church or not. Whatever your situation, in setting up a Spiritual Formation Group it is a good idea to start by praying about the matter, trusting God to guide you as you talk to people in your group about this possible new direction.

If the early signs are not positive you can relax and continue to appreciate your group for what it is for the time being. If the response is positive, you can start making plans either to adopt the format recommended here or simply to integrate individual aspects of the programme into your existing structure.

Starting a new group

Involve your church staff
If you want to start a group in your church, the expertise and encouragement of the pastor or priest and other leaders will be invaluable. Talking to them about your plans is not merely a common courtesy; it is essential if the plan is to have a positive effect on your church.

It is best if possible to sit down together and discuss the programme and any concerns thoroughly. The pastoral staff may have small group plans that currently do not include Spiritual Formation Groups. Try not to leave the meeting before reaching a consensus.

Most church leaders who have become acquainted with the programme have not only allowed groups to start, but have endorsed them, sometimes getting involved themselves.

Find one other person
The next step is to find at least one other person who is interested in such a group, perhaps a close friend or a person at your church. Your eagerness to start a group is invaluable. A positive attitude is infectious. But keep in mind that the group will not be for everyone.

Once you have found a partner, you have actually established a group. Many Spiritual Formation Groups involve only two people. But you may want to invite others.

Invite others to join you
Some people will be drawn by your excitement, others will simply be curious. Some will not feel comfortable ultimately so you should be prepared for this.

It is our experience, however, that many people would like to be in this kind of small group but may never have been asked to join one.

The following suggestions may help find people who are interested in experiencing growth in their spiritual journey:

- Put a notice in the church newsletter, bulletin or website.

- Make an announcement to the congregation or worship group.

- Send letters or emails and follow up with a telephone call.

Since this is your group, you can decide whom to meet with, where to meet, and when to begin. But like other decisions about the spiritual life, this one should be made only after careful, thoughtful prayer.

Find the right number

How many people should be in a Spiritual Formation Group? We recommend two to six (or maximum seven), though occasionally groups with as many as eight members meet successfully.

Our experience shows that when there are too many people in a group, either they go beyond the recommended time of one and one-and-a-half hours or some members do not have an opportunity to share.

Also, the level of intimacy decreases when groups become too large. People tend not to share in groups larger than five or six. A group composed of four to five people feels safer for most of us.

Once your group starts, others will hear about it and eventually more people may wish to join. Should the Spiritual Formation Group become too large, you could divide and form two or more smaller groups.

Some basic questions and answers

Q *What is a Spiritual Formation Group?*

A Most of us want to know in very simple terms what such a group will be about. You will be able to meet this enquiry once you have looked through and become familiar with the materials and plan presented in this book. A basic explanation can be found in the introduction or the following can be used (or adapted) to invite people to join the group:

During the next nine meetings we will be introduced to six dimensions of Christian discipleship – prayer, virtue, empowerment, compassion, proclamation, and wholeness – as seen in the life of Jesus Christ. We will also learn how we can practise the spiritual disciplines that flow from his life and, between each meeting, do at least one of them on our own. We will gather together and discuss our experiences, thereby learning what it means to encourage one another in our individual spiritual growth.

Q *What kind of commitment is expected?*

A The initial commitment is to an eight-session 'test-drive' plus one ordinary meeting. This is just a trial period. The group will meet for an hour to an hour and a half for nine sessions, preferably weekly or fortnightly. The schedule should be something that is agreeable to all participants.

At the end of the ninth meeting (or, if the group prefers, at a special tenth meeting) the participants will evaluate their experience and decide whether or not to continue gathering. This will help people who are not ready to make a lengthy commitment at the outset. Most of us like to test the water before diving in. After nine meetings the benefits – as well as the work involved – will be apparent. A responsible decision to commit to the group can then be made by each individual.

Q *Is there anything that should be brought to the meetings?*

A We recommend that each person has a copy of this workbook and a personal Bible so the group can work through the sessions together. Books can be made available at the first meeting or be given out in advance.

Q *Should groups be composed of only men or only women, or can they be mixed?*

A We have learned that the level of intimacy and sharing is much deeper and develops much quicker if group members are the same gender. Why? The more a group of people have in common, the more they can relate to each other. They share similar struggles and talk about them with fewer inhibitions.

Yet there is something to be said in favour of a mixed group (whether the mix is gender, age or background) with its added variety, broader spectrum of life experiences and differing perspectives. The makeup of the group is ultimately up to you.

Q *Can husbands and wives be in the same group?*

A Yes. But many groups that include husbands and wives report that participating together is a mixed blessing. It can be a tremendous way for a couple to grow closer, and it adds incentives in the area of mutual accountability. On the other hand, some people report struggling over what they should or should not share. Spouses may hesitate to share a private struggle, feeling that they should try to work it out on their own, thus preventing them from benefiting from the help of the group.

Numerous couples in fact form a Spiritual Formation Group by themselves. They meet regularly with each other to review how they are doing and to make plans for the future, sharing their joys and concerns with one another.

Whether husbands and wives should be in the same group depends upon what the individuals find the most beneficial.

Q *Is a Spiritual Formation Group for 'saints' only?*

A No. While the title may sound a bit ominous, Spiritual Formation Groups are designed to meet the needs of people who have little knowledge of the spiritual disciplines and minimal experience of doing them. The workbook uses a step-by-step approach to teach and model the disciplines, explaining the 'whats' and 'whys' and especially the 'hows'.

Does this mean the workbook is too easy for the more spiritually mature? No. The exercises that you will do are basic and foundational and meet you where you are. At the same time they challenge you to move ahead, to grow spiritually.

Q *What might happen in a Spiritual Formation Group?*

A There is nothing magical about Spiritual Formation Groups. They contain no secret formula and they offer no easy shortcuts. What they can do is initiate in you a renewed and deepening spiritual life.

SESSION ONE

Discovering a Balanced Vision of Christian Faith and Practice

THE LIFE OF JESUS CHRIST

At the outset

A good starting point for this and each of the following sessions is a time of silent prayer for about three minutes. This should be guided by the leader of the session and taken in turn at each meeting. The purpose of prayer is for members of the group to prepare themselves for the meeting by seeking God's blessing, help and guidance.

After the opening *prayer*, we move straight to a time of *sharing* and discussion. The *exercises* suggested below provide a basis for possible discussion, but they are optional and to some extent dependent on the time available. You could choose one or two, for example, rather than all three.

Another approach for this opening session would be for everyone to introduce themselves. If this is done briefly, there should still be time to look at one or more of the exercises which in themselves will help people get to know each other.

In each session, the suggestions for the time of sharing will be under the heading 'The Footprints of God'. The discussion pointers will normally refer to the previous meeting or to the time in between when people will have been reflecting on the issues raised or doing exercises of their own.

Later in each session, other topics are suggested for *discussion* which build on the relevant themes. It is helpful to interact and engage with this material as time permits, since doing so will deepen understanding and help everyone to get to know one another well. How far the discussions go will depend on time constraints and on the group's preferences.

In this first session, the suggested exercises illustrate the issue of balance in the Christian life.

The footprints of God

EXERCISE 1

Jesus Christ functions in four main ways in the Christian's life: Saviour, Teacher, Lord, and Friend.

In our relationship with him, each of us experiences some of these roles more powerfully than others.

Which aspect have you experienced the most ?

In which would you like to see yourself grow stronger?

EXERCISE 2

In the following list, where do you feel most at ease?

a. at work

b. with a group of close friends

c. playing sports

d. being at home in a garden or reading

e. with large groups of people

As a way to get to know each other in the group, say briefly what your answer says about you.

EXERCISE 3

There are six distinct aspects to Jesus' life and work as described in the Gospels: devotion to God, virtue in thought and action, empowerment by the Spirit, compassion towards everyone, proclamation of the good news of the gospel, and the integration of his spiritual and his ordinary life.

Which of these areas of Jesus' life are you most familiar with?

1. praying

2. striving against sin

3. ministering and healing in the power of the Spirit

4. showing compassion

5. proclaiming the good news and reading the Scriptures

6. bringing God into ordinary life

Understanding a balanced Christian life

The discussion will have shown how we are often quite familiar with one way God works in our lives but less so with others. Equally, we are often more aware of some aspects of Jesus' ministry at the expense of different ones. And we all have distinct 'comfort zones'.

In a group such as this, we will be challenged to stretch beyond what we know and have experienced already as Christians. Change can be unsettling, but holding too tightly to security keeps many of us from growing. Authentic spiritual growth requires that we venture out of our comfort zones and experience God in new and exciting ways. When we read the Gospels:

We see Jesus praying, and we listen to his teaching on the life of intimacy with God.

We see Jesus battling with Satan in the wilderness, and we listen to his teaching on the importance of a pure heart.

We see Jesus ministering in great power, and we listen to his teaching on the comfort, wisdom, and strength that come from the Holy Spirit.

We see Jesus helping the sick and the needy, and we listen to his teaching on the importance of caring for our neighbour.

We see Jesus proclaiming the good news of the kingdom of heaven, and we listen to him reading from the Scriptures.

We see Jesus integrate sacred and secular while observing the ceremonies of his faith.

From this life of Jesus Christ there emerge six distinct areas:

- devotion to God

- virtue in thought, word, and action

- empowerment by the Spirit

- compassion toward all people

- proclamation of the good news of the gospel

- integration between faith and work

This Spiritual Formation approach is based on the life of Jesus Christ. His life was balanced. We want to achieve the same balance in our lives.

Jesus Christ – the model of a balanced life

Different influences affect our spiritual lives. To achieve balance, we need to become aware of what influences us and where our response is strong or weak.

The history of the Church has also been marked by different traditions or 'movements', a word used to describe how God's Spirit moved upon individuals and groups of people with a particular mission. These movements, each bringing a focused renewal to the Church, reflect the six main aspects of Jesus' ministry. When one effort waned, a new movement emphasising another aspect tended to emerge.

The following examples illustrate these movements. Looking at them, and then doing the suggested exercise, can help us towards balance in our lives.

In the fourth century, men and women fled city life to found cloisters and monasteries where they emphasised the importance of solitude, meditation, and prayer. Antony of Egypt was an early leader of these 'Desert Mothers and Fathers'. The Church was strengthened by their emphasis upon intimacy with God, and **a contemplative movement** was born.

In the early eighteenth century, John Wesley and his friends formed a group nicknamed the 'Holy Club' and began focusing on moral laxity and the need for Christians to overcome sinful habits. They developed a 'method', and the Church once again took sin seriously. The purifying effects of the Methodist effort were dramatic, and it became **a holiness movement**.

In the seventeenth century the Church witnessed a new outbreak of the Holy Spirit in the lives of men and women who were called 'Quakers', led by the ministry of George Fox. The active presence of the Spirit in the lives of believers became the empowering principle behind scores of conversions. The active role of the Spirit was at the centre of their worship, and it propelled them into evangelism, missions, and social concern. This is an example of **a charismatic movement**.

In the late twelfth century Francis of Assisi and a group of followers abandoned their former lives and went about the Italian countryside, caring for the sick, the poor, and the lame. Countless men and women followed Francis's lead, forming the Franciscan and Poor Clare orders. Their impact on disease and poverty was remarkable. This is an example of **a social justice movement**.

In the sixteenth century Martin Luther and others proclaimed the gospel of Jesus Christ after discovering its message freshly in the Bible. This message of hope and victory was expressed by clergy and laity in sermons, mission efforts, and personal witnessing. In the history of the Church it is a wonderful example of **an evangelical movement**.

In the eighteenth century Count Nikolaus Ludwig von Zinzendorf allowed remnants of the persecuted Moravian Church (Unitas Fratum) to build the village of Herrnhut on his estate. Initially divided, the group became unified when they experienced a powerful outpouring of the Holy Spirit after Zinzendorf led them in daily Bible studies and in formulating the 'Brotherly Agreement'. The Moravians joyfully served God - praying, evangelising and helping other - in the midst of baking, teaching, weaving, and raising families. This is an example of **an incarnational movement**.

There have been other similar movements, both before and after the examples mentioned above, but certainly these stand out as efforts that had particularly dramatic effects upon the life and history of the Church.

Recognising our strengths

These movements illustrate six Traditions that continue to be apparent in the Church today. If one becomes dominant at the expense of the others, there is a danger of extremes and therefore of difficulties. Division and recrimination can so easily result. This is why we need all six Traditions functioning in our lives. Spiritual balance brings spiritual health.

EXERCISE 4

A wheel is formed by placing spokes around a centre hub. Each spoke must be equally strong and equally long in order for the wheel to function properly. If any spoke is too short, the wheel may roll, but will obviously thump with the effort, not functioning as it should. We, too, will feel the 'bumps' in our spiritual lives if one area is stonger than another, as this exercise will demonstrate.

Below is a diagram of the spokes of a wheel. Using a scale of 1 to 10 (with 1 being the least proficient and closest to the centre of the wheel) estimate where you are in each area on the wheel spokes. Place dots at those points, then connect the dots from spoke to spoke to form a ring around the hub.

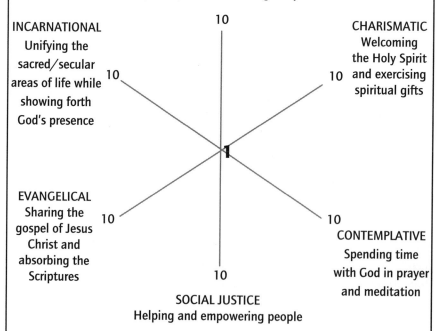

HOLINESS
Seeking purity and overcoming temptation

INCARNATIONAL
Unifying the sacred/secular areas of life while showing forth God's presence

CHARISMATIC
Welcoming the Holy Spirit and exercising spiritual gifts

EVANGELICAL
Sharing the gospel of Jesus Christ and absorbing the Scriptures

CONTEMPLATIVE
Spending time with God in prayer and meditation

SOCIAL JUSTICE
Helping and empowering people

This exercise is not about marks out of ten; it is about revealing where we can grow. God has touched each of our lives in important ways and has given us unique abilities and talents. For this we can rejoice and be thankful. Equally, we have areas of weakness in our lives. It is rare to find someone strong in all six areas!

Each person will be different, which is why meeting in a group is so fruitful: we can learn a lot from each other. The potential for growth is enormous so don't be discouraged. The excitement of this balanced strategy is in becoming strong in areas where we might previously have thought it impossible.

In the coming sessions, we will not only learn about the Traditions in more detail, but we will also discover simple ways to begin working their accompanying disciplines into our lives.

> ## AN EXERCISE TO TAKE AWAY FROM THE MEETING
> Take a few minutes during the coming week to write a brief 'letter to God'. In this letter, try to recall the first time you sensed God's presence and some of the ways God has revealed himself to you since then. Close the letter by giving thanks for all that you know of God now and for all that you would like to know in the the future. The letter should be about one page in length, and it will be shared (if you choose) at the beginning of the next week's gathering.

Ending and beginning

It is good to end each session in quiet and prayerful unity.

Passing the Peace: one suggestion is to speak or pray specific words of affirmation to one another, mentioning gratefully what God has done in each person's life.

Secondly, praying the Lord's Prayer together is simple and powerful. This is the suggested conclusion to every session. You can choose which version to use. Below are two, one of which is Dallas Willard's version found in his book *The Divine Conspiracy*. Whichever version you go for, it is helpful to pray out loud, together, joining hands if you like.

> *Our Father, who art in heaven*
> *hallowed be thy name.*
> *Thy kingdom come,*
> *thy will be done*
> *on earth as it is in heaven.*
> *Give us this day our daily bread,*
> *and forgive us our trespasses*
> *as we forgive those who trespass against us.*
> *And lead us not into temptation*

but deliver us from evil.
For thine is the kingdom, the power and the glory,
for ever and ever. Amen

Dear Father always near us,
May your name be treasured and loved,
May your rule be completed in us –
May your will be done here on earth
In just the way it is done in heaven
Give us today the things we need today,
And forgive us our sins and impositions on you
As we are forgiving all who in any way offend us.
Please don't put us through trials,
But deliver us from everything bad.
Because you are the one in charge,
And you have all the power,
And the glory too is all yours – forever –
Which is just the way we want it!

The Divine Conspiracy, p.269 (HarperCollins, 1998)

Dallas Willard says of his suggested alternative to 'Amen': ' "Just the way we want it" is not a bad paraphrase for "amen." What is needed at the end of this great prayer is a ringing affirmation of the goodness of God and God's world. If your nerves can take it, you might (occasionally?) try "Whoopee!" I imagine God himself will not mind.'

At the end of this and every session, you will need to establish who will facilitate the next meeting. The job is not onerous: minimum preparation is required, since the structure and guidelines for each meeting are clear. Someone different should volunteer each time.

SESSION TWO

Practising the Prayer-Filled Life

THE CONTEMPLATIVE TRADITION

As with all sessions, we open with a time of silent prayer.

The footprints of God

> ### GROUP DISCUSSION
>
> Beginning with the leader for this meeting, tell each other how you got on with the 'Letter to God', the exercise from last time.
>
> Some will be happy to read their letter out. Others may wish to share only one or two things. Others may not have felt able to write a letter, or may not want to share what was written.
>
> The question to be asked of everyone in the group, as the basis for discussion, is 'What did I learn about God and about myself from doing this exercise?'

Jesus and prayer

In each session, we are going to look at one aspect of Jesus' life, and see how it gives rise to one of the six Traditions.

In this session, we look briefly at what is revealed in the Bible about Jesus' prayer life.

Mark 14.32–36 to be read aloud by one member of the group.

They went to a place called Gethsemane; and [Jesus] said to his disciples, 'Sit here while I pray.' He took with him Peter and James and John, and began to be distressed and agitated. And said to them, 'I am deeply grieved, even to death, remain here, and keep awake.' And going a little farther, he threw himself on the ground and prayed that, if it were possible, the hour might pass from him. He said, 'Abba, Father, for you all things are possible. Remove this cup from me; yet, not what I want, but what you want.'

GROUP DISCUSSION

What impresses you about this passage? Why do you think Jesus prayed that God 'remove the cup' from him, the cup symbolising his destiny to die on the Cross?

Thinking it through

This section, 'Thinking it Through', is a resource in each session to help the group appreciate more of the named passage. As with later sections, here and in other chapters, it can be read aloud or summarised by the leader. People can also refer back to any material in the workbook at a later stage.

Jesus was a person of prayer who had an intimate relationship with the Father. He prayed regularly and he prayed often and he addressed God as 'Abba, Father'. The word 'Abba' is similar to our word 'Daddy'. It indicates closeness, love, a trusting relationship. Jesus was not afraid to talk with God, to share his fears and his anguish. In the Garden of Gethsemane – at his moment of greatest need – Jesus prays. His prayer is full of faith: 'For you all things are possible.' His prayer is honest: 'Remove this cup from me.' In the end, his prayer expresses a desire to do the will of God: 'Yet, not what I want, but what you want.'

Many other passages tell us how important prayer was to Jesus (the following references can be looked up independently of this session).

- Even though he was very busy, he took time to talk with God (Mark 1.35; 6.46; Matthew 14.22-25; Luke 6.12-13).

- He said that he could do nothing apart from God and that his entire mission in life was to do the will of God (John 5.19).

- He frequently left the crowds to be alone with God, retreating to 'a quiet place' to pray (Mark 1.35).

- He became a role model for the disciples; when they looked at Jesus, they longed to be like him, to have the same kind of intimacy with God that he had. That is why they said, 'Lord, teach us to pray' (Luke 11.1).

A God of compassion

In each session, we look at what each aspect of Jesus' life also teaches us about God.

Jesus prays to the Father because he knows God's nature – loving, giving, forgiving. Jesus tells us that God knows our needs even before we ask him (Matthew 6.8). Jesus describes (and demonstrates in his own life) a God of compassion.

The most vivid picture of God's tender love comes in the story of the Prodigal Son (read Luke 15.11–32). A wayward son who has squandered his father's money, his own inheritance, returns in repentance and remorse, expecting judgement and punishment. Instead he receives a loving welcome and a warm embrace.

This is God's nature. If we knew God in this way, praying and talking with him would not be a chore or a duty, but would rather be our inner desire throughout the day. God longs for us to respond to his self-sacrificing love. Once we catch a glimpse of what God is like, we will want to spend time with him.

> ### GROUP DISCUSSION
> The father in the story of the Prodigal Son gives us a snapshot of the nature of God. How does this picture match your own understanding of what God is like?

The Contemplative Tradition

At the heart of each Tradition or Stream is God. Jesus is 'God with us', a physical presence to show us what God is like. His actions and words reveal God's nature to us. When we practise 'the prayer-filled life', or the Contemplative Tradition, we discover the tender love of God.

From Jesus we see, hear, and learn about God's nature. Because he knew what God is like Jesus frequently spent time with him in solitude and in prayer and these two factors – the nature of God and the practice of Jesus – gave birth to 'the Contemplative Tradition'. It is a historic stream within the life of the Church that Jesus himself modelled for us.

Our lives are busy, often full of worries. Practising the disciplines of the Contemplative Stream equips us to create in our lives the 'space' that God longs for and the 'intimacy' that we need. Most of us live in the midst of jobs and families and responsibilities that hamper our efforts to spend time with God. And everything in our hurry-scurry culture works against our efforts to set aside time for him. Colleges and businesses provide courses in time management so that we can squeeze every drop from every minute. Televisions bombard us with ads that tempt us to spend our 'leisure time' shopping or attending movies or eating out.

We all agree that it is very difficult to make space for God in our day and in our culture, and yet we need times of solitude and silence, times of contemplation and reflection, times of prayer and meditation. We need these times – just as much as Jesus needed them – to gain strength and wisdom and compassion. All three qualities flow from the space, the room we make for God in our lives.

Practising the Contemplative Tradition

The following list includes ways in which we can begin to enter this life of intimacy with God, or the 'prayer-filled life'. They might be called 'spiritual disciplines' or 'spiritual exercises'. As such, they are activities we do that open us to God's presence.

These exercises, given at the end of this and every session, are intended to be done in your own time, at home or somewhere where you can be focused and present with God. It is often difficult to get round to this, and it takes time to find a rhythm which suits you. Persevere, however, trusting God for help. Experience is the best teacher. Keep in mind that these are only a sample of many exercises that will help you enter into the contemplative life.

Three simple precautions:

- First, do not be afraid to fail. To reach a goal is not the reason you do a spiritual discipline; it is to experience God. Even in failure you are learning and experiencing new and valuable things.

- Second, keep your emphasis on God, not on the method. It is hard initially, but try to think about why you are doing an exercise rather than what you are doing.

- Third, feel free to modify the exercise to fit your needs. In the first session we looked at our areas of strengths and weaknesses. You may be strong in this area – the prayer-filled life – or you may be weak. Change the exercise to fit your present need.

EXERCISES IN THE CONTEMPLATIVE TRADITION

Each person should choose one of the following exercises and practise it several times before the next meeting. If possible, look at the exercises together before the end of this session.

1. Set aside five to ten minutes each day for prayer.

2. Find a time in your schedule that is free of interruption when you can turn your thoughts to God.

You may want to read a Bible verse and meditate on it, or you may want to spend the time talking with God about your needs and concerns. The idea is simply to set aside your busy activities (or not start them), and to turn your attention to God.

3. Spend five to ten minutes each day in silence.

Carve out a time that is free from interruption, and use this time to be silent. While letting silence and its peace wash over you, pray without words. Very close friends can communicate without words; try this with God. Simply enjoy God's presence, God's loving arms wrapped around you.

4. Read selections from a devotional book.

Find a book on the spiritual life that interests you. It may be a spiritual classic, like St. Augustine's *Confessions*, or it may be a devotional classic, like Oswald Chambers' *My Utmost for His Highest*. However, instead of reading what you select simply to understand it, read it 'with God', knowing that God is there in the room with you. Discover God in the reading.

5. Pray the same prayer for ten minutes each day.

There is a tradition in the Eastern Church called 'hesychasm', which is the practice of repeating a simple prayer over and over. The main idea is to focus our thoughts on God so that God can enter into our hearts. You might like to try the 'hesychastic' prayer, 'Lord Jesus Christ, Son of God, have mercy on me', or use a verse from a psalm – perhaps 'Create in me a clean heart, O God' (Psalm 51.10).

6. Write an original prayer.

Take time to write a prayer as if it were a 'letter to God'. Beginning with 'Dear God', tell God your hopes and dreams, your worries, your needs. You may even want to confess your sins and to ask for forgiveness. Most important, use the prayer to open the lines of communication between yourself and God. Do not write the prayer as though it will be read by others one day. Like a personal journal, keep your prayer confidential so that you have the freedom to be honest. Once you have written it, read and pray it every day until our next gathering.

Ending and beginning

We end with prayers of affirmation, peace and brief intercession, and then the Lord's Prayer, spoken together (see Session One p.29, or the Order of Meeting p.82, for the Lord's Prayer).

A member of the group needs to volunteer to facilitate the next meeting. It is good to take it in turns to lead the group.

SESSION THREE

Practising the Virtuous Life

THE HOLINESS TRADITION

We open with silent prayer.

The footprints of God

> ## GROUP DISCUSSION
> How did everyone get on with the spiritual exercises undertaken during the week? What did people learn about God and about themselves?

Jesus and virtue

When Jesus was tested in the wilderness by the devil, he remained true to his mission and emerged pure from the experience.

Matthew 4.1–11 to be read aloud by one member of the group.

> Then Jesus was led up by the Spirit into the wilderness to be tempted by the devil. He fasted forty days and forty nights, and afterwards he was famished. The tempter came and said to him, 'If you are the Son of God, command these stones to become loaves of bread.' But he answered, 'It is written,
> "One does not live by bread alone,
> but by every word that comes from the mouth of God." '
> Then the devil took him to the holy city and placed him on the pinnacle of the temple, saying, 'If you are the Son of God, throw yourself down; for it is written,
> "He will command his angels concerning you," and "On their hands they will bear you up,

so that you will not dash your foot against a stone." '
Jesus said to him, 'Again it is written, "Do not put the Lord your God to the test." '

Again, the devil took him to a very high mountain and showed him all the kingdoms of the world and their splendour; and he said to him, 'All these I will give you, if you will fall down and worship me.' Jesus said to him, 'Away with you Satan! For it is written,
"Worship the Lord your God,
and serve only him.'" '
Then the devil left him and suddenly angels came and waited on him.

GROUP DISCUSSION

Why did Jesus not yield to any of these temptations? Have you ever been tempted with an offer that was hard to refuse?

Thinking it through

Jesus' baptism (Matthew 3.13–17) comes right before his testing in the wilderness. This is important because at the conclusion of his baptism a 'voice from heaven' proclaims that Jesus is 'my Son' (Matthew 3.17). Exactly who Jesus is has just been confirmed and now the devil will do everything he can to destroy Jesus.

Notice that it was 'the Spirit' who led Jesus into the wilderness 'to be tempted'. This may seem odd to us: how could God instigate Jesus' temptation? The word translated as 'to be tempted' actually means 'to be tested'. There is a subtle but important difference. God tests; the devil tempts. God does not want Jesus to fail; the devil does. The Spirit leads Jesus into the wilderness to fast and to pray and to resist the forces that will assault him during his mission. Having overcome them, he is ready for his journey toward the Cross.

There are three temptations: turn stones into bread, leap off the temple roof to see if angels will come to the rescue, and acquire all of the kingdoms in the world. The first two temptations challenge Jesus to prove his deity: 'If you are the Son of God . . .'; the last temptation dares Jesus to reject his deity. Jesus rebukes all three by quoting from the Hebrew Scriptures (Deuteronomy 8.3; 6.16; 6.13). The devil shows that he, too, knows the Scriptures as he tries to make the second temptation more appealing by quoting from Psalm 91 (v. 11.12). However, Jesus knows better, and he cannot be tricked. In the end the devil leaves because he has been unable to entice Jesus to sin.

God cares about holiness

What is sin? According to the Bible sin is rejecting the commandments of God.

We might be accustomed to thinking of God's commandments as rules that stifle our happiness and simply make us feel guilty. The opposite is true. Take, for example, the Ten Commandments (Exodus 20.1–21). Each commandment calls us to the blessed life, the pathway to true happiness. The seventh commandment, 'Thou shalt not commit adultery', may seem to restrict our sexual freedom. In reality, the opposite is true. To engage in an adulterous affair leads to pain and loneliness; to remain faithful to our spouse brings true freedom. God knows this. Holiness is something God wishes for us simply because it is the best way to live. The commandments of God are not meant to make our lives a dull drudgery, but to make them whole and full. They are given to us so that we might live abundantly.

God's plan completes and integrates our lives; sin disrupts and fragments our lives. While sin seems appealing on the surface, it is ultimately destructive. We find that it offers a short season of delight and a long, sometimes lifelong, season of pain. God knows that we are drawn to sin, and prescribes a way of living that helps us resist it. Living a holy life is not limited to 'super saints'; rather, it is healthy and functional for everyone.

GROUP DISCUSSION

What examples can you think of that demonstrate sin's destructive power?

What is the Holiness Tradition?

To trust and obey is at the heart of the Holiness Tradition.

Jesus said, 'If you wish to enter into life, keep the commandments' (Matthew 19.17). We do not refer to the commandments as the 'Ten Suggestions', as if they were hints to help us improve ourselves. Keeping the commandments is mandatory, and God provides a way to obey them; yielding our lives to him.

Obedience is the natural outgrowth of loving and trusting God like a child loves and trusts a parent. We do not obey God's commands grudgingly; instead, we keep them willingly because our experience with God proves that obeying his commands is our best course of action.

But holiness or purity of heart is not merely obeying certain rules. Jesus openly challenged the division among the Israelites, and the Pharisees in particular, between inward purity and outward ritual. 'What goes into your mouth does not make you "unclean", but what comes out of your mouth, that is what makes you "unclean" ' (Matthew 15.11, NIV). Jesus turns our attention away from ritual purity and points to purity of heart from which flows unshakable obedience to God (Matthew 5.8).

As we shall see, trusting and obeying manifest themselves in our lives in many ways.

Practising the Holiness Tradition

Since God desires that we become holy, it is our task to find ways to do this.

When we engage in certain disciplines, we are not instantly holy, nor have we suddenly completed a task that is rewarded by a merit badge of godliness. Rather, we engage in certain disciplines and exercises as a means of training, much like an athlete trains to become more proficient at a particular sport.

The result of doing the following exercises is a greater ability to obey God's commandments. We become able to do that which we were unable to do; able to keep commandments we were unable to keep.

For example, two of the following exercises help discipline the tongue. If I tell myself simply to stop saying negative things, I will likely fail. But if I begin with the 'inside', praying for a pure heart and then committing to watch my words, I have opened the door to the Spirit to begin helping me. When I am about to say something negative, the Spirit speaks a word of caution to me, and that blessed split second makes change in my behaviour possible.

The result is not 'Wow, aren't I special because I stopped saying negative things!' (which sounds much like the Pharisee in Jesus' parable in Luke 18.9–14), but rather, 'God is beginning to mould and shape my life.'

Remembering the difference between working from the inside out, rather than from the outside in, is extremely important when practising these disciplines.

EXERCISES IN THE HOLINESS TRADITION

Look at the following exercises together before the end of this session.
Each person should choose one to do during the coming week or fortnight.

1. Pray for the Holy Spirit to purify your heart and mind; then listen.

God works from the inside out, and he works via the Holy Spirit to bring
about change. Set aside a substantial amount of time (say, one hour)
for a deep and heartfelt prayer. During that time, ask God to purify your
heart and mind through the power of the Holy Spirit. The key to the
effectiveness of your prayer will be your willingness to surrender control of
your life to God. Ask God to search your heart to see if there is any hidden
evil in your life or any activity that God wants you to stop. Then listen.
When you have a sense of what God wants to free you from, pray that the
Spirit will purge that sin – even the desire for it – from your life. Holiness
is born in prayers like these.

2. Respond to temptation with the word of God.

Jesus overcame the devil's temptations by holding fast to God's
commandments. Memorise those three responses (Deuteronomy 8.3;
6.16; 6.13), and when you are tempted by the enemy to (1) gratify
selfish desires, (2) doubt God's power, or (3) seek wealth, power, or fame,
respond to the temptation with the corresponding verse of Scripture. Jesus
used the power of God through Scripture to defeat the devil, and so can
we.

3. Try a twenty-four-hour, partial fast.

Jesus fasted in the wilderness to gain spiritual strength. When we fast,
we are saying 'no' to the uncontrolled appetites of our body and thereby
gaining mastery over them. The practice of fasting also reveals hidden
things – anger, selfishness, inability to delay gratification, laziness, and
so on – which can become areas for change (and growth) in the future. A
simple way to begin is to fast from lunch to lunch, skipping dinner and
breakfast in between. After eating lunch on the first day, do not eat a full
meal until lunch on the second day. During the twenty-four hours drink
plenty of water, and at mealtimes drink a glass of fruit juice if you want.
Remember, in the fasting you are 'feasting' upon God.

4. Two disciplines for 'taming the tongue'.

What we say reveals what is in our hearts. That is why Jesus said that it is
not what goes into the mouth but what comes out that makes a person

unclean (Matthew 15.11). In other words, what we say makes us 'unclean'.

James also reminds us of the power of words (James 3.5–12). Like fire, they can refine or destroy. The following disciplines will help you monitor the things you say and gain some control over the awesome power of the tongue.

a. *Go a day without saying anything negative.*
In the morning, ask the Holy Spirit to put a guard over your mouth (Psalm 141.3), preventing you from saying anything negative. Be ruthless about this! Do not let even the slightest hint of criticism or judgement come out of your mouth. You may find yourself in situations that call for an honest appraisal, for example, when asked what you think of something. Be honest, but do not be critical. Instead, search for ways to be positive about everything around you and be ready to give compliments as often as you can.

b. *Go a day without saying anything that is dishonest.*
Jesus said of Nathaniel said that he was a person without 'guile' (John 1.47, KJV). What a compliment! Guile is dishonesty, deceit, speaking falsehood, shading the truth, manipulating words, double-talk, and the like. Pray that the Spirit will make your heart pure and honest and ask for a 'guard' to be placed over your mouth that will alert you to anything that is less than honest and forthright. Do not manipulate your words; let your 'yes' be 'yes' and your 'no' be 'no'.

In both of these activities you will find a great sense of release. Our words hurt not only others, but ourselves too. When we say negative things, it affects our spirit. The old adage says 'When we throw mud, we can't help but get some on ourselves'. We find freedom and peace when we begin taming the tongue.

Ending and beginning

We end with prayer for one another, and say the Lord's Prayer together, before deciding who will lead the next meeting.

SESSION FOUR

Practising the Spirit-Empowered Life

THE CHARISMATIC TRADITION

We open with silent prayer.

The footprints of God

GROUP DISCUSSION

How did everyone get on with the spiritual exercises undertaken during the week? What did people learn about God and about themselves?

Jesus and the Holy Spirit

The verses we are about to look at from the Gospel of John are known by biblical scholars as the five Paraclete Sayings. They describe the origin, character, and work of the Holy Spirit.

The word translated as 'advocate', which Jesus uses to describe the Holy Spirit in these verses, is from the Greek word 'paraclete'. It originally meant 'advocate' in the legal sense; one who pleads a client's case before a court. The root of the word means 'to call alongside', which denotes the helping character of the Holy Spirit.

John 14.15-17, 25-26; 15.26-27; 16.7-15 to be read aloud, perhaps by different people in the group.

'If you love me you will keep my commandments. And I will ask the Father, and he will give you another Advocate, to be with you for ever. This is the Spirit of truth, whom the world cannot receive because it neither sees him

or knows him. You know him because he abides with you, and he will be in you.' (John 14.15-17)

'I have said these things to you while I am still with you. But the Advocate, the Holy Spirit, whom the Father will send in my name, will teach you everything, and remind you of all that I have said to you.' (John 14.25-26)

'When the Advocate comes, whom I will send to you from the Father, the Spirit of truth who comes from the Father, he will testify on my behalf. You also are to testify because you have been with me from the beginning.' (John 15.26-27)

'Nevertheless, I tell you the truth: it is to your advantage that I go away, for if I do not go away, the Advocate will not come to you; but if I go, I will send him to you. And when he comes, he will prove the world wrong about sin and righteousness and judgement: about sin, because they do not believe in me; about righteousness, because I am going to the Father and you will see me no longer; about judgement, because the ruler of this world has been condemned.

'I still have many things to say to you, but you cannot bear them now. When the Spirit of truth comes, he will guide you into all the truth; for he will not speak on his own, but will speak whatever he hears, and he will declare to you the things that are to come. He will glorify me, because he will take what is mine and declare it to you. All that the Father has is mine. For this reason I said that he will take what is mine and declare it to you.' (John 16.7-15)

GROUP DISCUSSION

How do you understand the Holy Spirit's work in your own life?

Thinking it through

When Jesus tells his disciples that he must leave them, he directs them not to worry or to be afraid because he is going to ask the Father to send the Spirit to be their advocate, their helper:

- The Holy Spirit is the Spirit of truth. He affirms what is good and pure and true and holy.

- The Holy Spirit functions as a teacher: he teaches believers 'everything'. Like our earthly teachers, the Spirit reminds us and corrects us.

- The Holy Spirit functions as a witness who 'testifies' to Jesus Christ. When we hear the gospel, the 'good news' that Jesus Christ was born, lived, died, and rose from the dead, the Holy Spirit witnesses to our spirit that it is true and prompts us to accept the good news.

- In addition to being an advocate who defends believers, the Holy Spirit is a prosecutor who will 'prove the world wrong' about its relationship to God; particularly about 'sin, righteousness, and judgment'. We must always remember that it is the Spirit's task to convict, not ours.

- The Holy Spirit does not speak on his own but only 'whatever he hears' from the Father. He speaks of what is to come, gives honour to the Son, and passes on the things of Christ and God to the believer: 'He will take what is mine and declare it to you. All that the Father has is mine.'

The departure of Christ meant sorrow for the disciples, but Jesus pointed out to them that 'it is to your advantage that I go away'. His departure was necessary in order for the Holy Spirit to come and and begin a new stage in the work of God, enabling his people to become members of Christ's spiritual body and empowering them for ministry.

God the Father, Son and Holy Spirit

The Holy Spirit has been called the forgotten person of the Trinity. Since its beginning on the day of Pentecost, the Church has believed in one God comprised of three persons – 'God the Father, God the Son, and God the Holy Spirit' – but the Holy Spirit, an equal in the Trinity, is often neglected. We pray to God the Father in the name and authority of Jesus, the Son, and forget the role of the Holy Spirit in our lives.

This is tragic. From the standpoint of God (as seen through the words of Jesus), the Holy Spirit is God, and in particular God at work in the Christian. What God the Father and God the Son began, God the Spirit continues and completes. In Michelangelo's famous painting on the ceiling of the Sistine Chapel, God is reaching out his life-giving hand to Adam, and Adam is extending his hand in response. However, their fingers never quite touch. The Holy Spirit is this missing touch of God. The distance between God and his people is bridged by the Holy Spirit so that we actually become one with God.

It is through the person of the Holy Spirit, an equal in the Trinity, that God works in the believer.

As believers, we are temples in whom the Holy Spirit dwells (see 1 Corinthians 3.16; 6.19; 2 Corinthians 6.16). God has chosen to empower through the Spirit those who witness about Christ, and to convict and convince those who listen to them. He has chosen to endow men and women, through the power of the Spirit, with specific abilities or gifts that build the body of Christ, or his Church (1 Corinthians 12.1, 8–11).

Most of all, he has chosen to cultivate the gospel soil of people's lives so that they bear spiritual fruit: love, joy, peace, patience, gentleness, goodness, faithfulness, meekness, self-control (Galatians 5.22). Without the fruit of the Spirit, the special gifts are like a 'clanging cymbal' that makes noise but has no value (1 Corinthians 13.1–3).

GROUP DISCUSSION

Of the Holy Spirit's fruit, listed above, which has matured in your life? Which has yet to bloom and grow?

What is the Charismatic Tradition?

The Charismatic Tradition reminds us that the Holy Spirit is absolutely essential in the Christian life.

The Spirit spurs the believer to pray and meditate (the focus of the Contemplative Tradition); to seek a virtuous life (the Holiness Tradition); to exercise mercy and compassion (the Social Justice Tradition); to proclaim the gospel as found in the Scriptures (the Evangelical Tradition), and to promote harmony between our faith and our work (the Incarnational Tradition).

However, it is not unusual for people to try to become faithful disciples on their own, without the power of the Holy Spirit. The vital, exciting, electrifying work of the Holy Spirit may be missing in our lives. Our struggle with temptation and sin and of our failure to live joyful lives could be traced to an unwillingness to welcome the Holy Spirit.

The word 'charismatic' comes from the Greek word 'charism' which means 'gift'. Charismatic movements have always demonstrated the active work of God in people's lives in ways that make others envious or distrustful. We should note that the Charismatic Tradition (like the other Traditions) is often characterised by excess and sham. This has led many in the Church to split away, which is regrettable.

God, as Spirit, dwells in each of us. God wants to be active in our lives; to endow us with supernatural abilities; to see us live with love, joy and peace. All of us should be able to give testimony to the work of the Holy Spirit in our lives – not just those who are 'charismatic' or 'pentecostal'.

It is our job to surrender ourselves to the energising work of the living God and to engage in activities that enable the Spirit to equip and empower us.

Practising the Charismatic Tradition

The Holy Spirit is received, not grasped. We cannot coerce or bribe the Holy Spirit. In fact, many of our efforts only impede the work of the Spirit. In this sense, practising the disciplines of the Charismatic Tradition is different from practising those of the other five Traditions.

To experience the ministry of the Holy Spirit, we begin by doing two things. First,we ask for the Holy Spirit (Luke 11.13). God waits for us to pray for the Spirit before he sends the One whose presence is a gift to those who simply ask. Second, we practise the discipline of waiting (Psalm 40.1).

When we pray for the Spirit, we are not praying for an answer; we are asking God to enter us, to fill us with his presence, his thoughts, his words. This requires the kind of passion that takes the form of patient waiting.

What kinds of things can we expect when the Holy Spirit begins to work in our lives? While it is true that the Lord works in mysterious ways, the Bible notes several functions of the Spirit in our lives. The following list may give you a few ideas of what we can expect to see happening within our hearts and minds:

The Holy Spirit:
- gives us a sense of our unity with Christ

- leads us into all truth

- helps us worship God

- guides our decision making

- illuminates our Bible study

- motivates us to action

- gives us the right words as we share our faith with others

- softens the minds and hearts of those with whom we share our faith.

These are works of the Spirit all of us can expect to see in our lives as we open ourselves to him.

As you do your chosen exercise this week, be sensitive to the inner attitudes, thoughts, and feelings you are experiencing. You will most likely see God at work in ways you have never noticed before.

One final caution: do not expect dramatic results or instant change. While there are many genuine works of the Holy Spirit that are immediate and life changing, these experiences are the exception, not the rule. The Spirit works primarily in our minds by shaping the way we think, and this takes time. For example, I may pray, 'Lord, give me patience—and give it to me now!' While I may desperately want to be patient, it will take time for this fruit of the Spirit to blossom and grow in my life. The fact that I desire to have more patience shows me that the Spirit is already at work, and it is my task to begin doing things that will develop the fruit. Genuine change takes time.

EXERCISES IN THE CHARISMATIC TRADITION

Each person should choose one of the following exercises and practise it before the next meeting. Look at the exercises together before the end of this session.

1. Yield to the work of the Spirit.

Spend one hour in prayer this week, specifically asking for the Spirit to begin working in your life in a new and powerful way. Remember, you are seeking God. Make no demands; have no expectations. Your only task is to surrender yourself to God, to open the door so the Spirit can come in and begin changing the way you think and live. This may lead to a time of confession.

2. Nurture the fruit of the Spirit.

Galatians 5.22 lists nine virtues called the fruit of the Spirit: love, joy, peace, patience, kindness, generosity, faithfulness, gentleness, and self-control. They are listed in contrast with the works of the flesh: fornication, impurity, licentiousness, idolatry, sorceries, enmities, strife, jealousy, anger, and so on (Galatians 5.19-21). While the fruit of the Spirit slips in unawares, Paul says we are responsible for living by the Spirit and keeping in step with the Spirit, which helps the fruit grow (Galatians 5.25).

Set aside fifteen minutes a day to meditate on the fruit of the Spirit. Ask God to show you which virtue needs to be more evident in your life.

Then ask the Holy Spirit to begin working in your mind and heart, knowing that change will come through sustained communion with God.

3. Discover your spiritual gifts.

One Corinthians 12.8–11 lists nine gifts of the Spirit: wisdom, knowledge, faith, healing, miraculous powers, prophecy, discernment, speaking in tongues, and the interpretation of tongues. Some people have argued that some of these particular gifts are no longer needed in the Church, but most feel that the Church still needs them. Explore these gifts through prayer, asking God to guide you to a gift (or perhaps more than one) that may be neglected and needs to be stirred up in your life or the life of your church fellowship (1 Timothy 4.14).

Read the Scriptures that refer to spiritual gifts, beginning with Romans 12.6–8, 1 Corinthians 12–14.25, and Ephesians 4.11–13. Ask in your church or among your friends for a recommendation of a good Christian book on the subject. Stay open to God's desire to build up, heal, and minister to the Church in all her expressions.

4. Read the Scriptures with the Holy Spirit.

The Holy Spirit opens our minds when we read the Bible, making us receptive to its message. More specifically, the Spirit helps us understand what the text is saying to us personally and applies its message to our particular situation. Select a passage from the Bible to reflect on. As you read, ask the Holy Spirit to highlight a specific verse or word that is specifically meant for you to hear. When you have discovered what God wants you to hear, spend ten to fifteen minutes reflecting on why it has impressed you and what lesson you need to learn from it.

5. Listen to the Advocate when making decisions.

One of the most important and basic ministries of the Holy Spirit is to provide guidance (Romans 8.14, Galatians 5.25). Do you need to make an important decision? Seek the Spirit – your Advocate – to help you. Take your concern to God in prayer. Ask God to give you direction, insight, leading. It may be an intuitive sense; it may be a friend's advice that you sense comes from God; or it may be a door of opportunity opening or closing. In all decisions, test the Spirit by examining the Scriptures. The Spirit of God will never lead you into a decision that is contrary to the principles and commandments found in the Bible.

Ending and beginning

We end with prayer for one another, and say the Lord's Prayer together, before deciding who will lead the next meeting.

SESSION FIVE

Practising the Compassionate Life

THE SOCIAL JUSTICE TRADITION

We open with silent prayer.

The footprints of God

GROUP DISCUSSION

How did everyone get on with the spiritual exercises undertaken during the week? What did people learn about God and about themselves?

Jesus and the Compassionate Life

Matthew 25.31–46 to be read aloud

> 'When the Son of Man comes in his glory, and all the angels with him, then he will sit on the throne of his glory. All the nations will be gathered before him, and he will separate people one from another as a shepherd separates the sheep from the goats, and he will put the sheep at his right hand and the goats at the left. Then the king will say to those at his right hand, "Come, you that are blessed by my Father, inherit the kingdom prepared for you from the foundation of the world; for I was hungry and you gave me food, I was thirsty and you gave me something to drink, I was a stranger and you welcomed me, I was naked and you gave me clothing, I was sick and you took care of me, I was in prison and you visited me." Then the righteous will answer him, "Lord, when was it that we saw you hungry and gave you food, or thirsty and gave you something to drink? And when was it that we saw you a stranger and welcomed you, or naked

and gave you clothing? And when was it that we saw you sick or in prison and visited you?" And the king will answer them, "Truly I tell you, just as you did it to one of the least of these who are members of my family, you did it to me." Then he will say to those at his left hand, "You that are accursed, depart from me into the eternal fire prepared for the devil and his angels; for I was hungry and you gave me no food, I was thirsty and you gave me nothing to drink, I was a stranger and you did not welcome me, naked and you did not give me clothing, sick and in prison and you did not visit me." Then they also will answer, "Lord, when was it that we saw you hungry or thirsty or a stranger or naked or sick or in prison, and did not take care of you?" Then he will answer them, "Truly I tell you, just as you did not do it to one of the least of these, you did not do it to me." And these will go away into eternal punishment, but the righteous into eternal life.'

GROUP DISCUSSION

What is this passage about? Judgement, compassion, love? All three?

Can you relate to one or more of the examples given of needy people, such as being a stranger? Describe what that was like.

Thinking it through

This passage is a powerful indictment of those who neglect the needy. It may seem like a parable in some ways, but it actually describes the future judgment of all the nations. Jesus, like a shepherd, will separate all people into two groups: those who cared for the needy and those who did not.

One detail about the judgment stands out starkly: Jesus tells his listeners – to their surprise – that when they have (or have not) cared for the needy, they have (or have not), cared for *him*. In serving those in need, we serve Jesus.

We also note that both groups call Jesus 'Lord'. But in Matthew 7.21 Jesus says, 'Not everyone who says to me, "Lord, Lord", will enter the kingdom of heaven, but only the one who does the will of my Father in heaven.' The judgment standard is not that they recognise Jesus as Lord, but rather that they do the will of God by meeting the physical and spiritual needs of Jesus' family.

We may be tempted to turn this teaching about doing good deeds into an obligation, or law. Here we must be careful. Martin Luther said that 'Christ did not free us from the law; he freed us from a wrong understanding of the law.' The 'wrong understanding' that Luther refers to is the belief that we can restore our relationship with God by doing good works. Christ frees us from these soul-killing notions. But the fact that we have been saved by grace through faith, 'and this is not your own doing; it is the gift of God' (Ephesians 2.8) increases our responsibility. We are not free to neglect the needy. Jesus told his disciples about the final judgement, and the account has been passed on to warn us that he expects more, not less, from those who call him Lord.

God and social justice

God cares deeply about how we treat one another.

When asked about the Law, Jesus responded by highlighting two key commandments: '"You shall love the Lord your God with all your heart, and with all your soul, and with all your mind." This is the greatest and first commandment. And a second is like it: "You shall love your neighbour as yourself." On these two commandments hang all the law and the prophets."' (Matthew 22.37–40)

The call to love one another is grounded in God's love for us. God loves us, so we should also love one another (1 John 4.11). Jesus, too, said, 'Just as I have loved you, you also should love one another' (John 13.34).

From God's perspective, each and every human being is a precious work of God. The book of Proverbs tells us, 'Those who oppress the poor insult their Maker, but those who are kind to the needy honour him' (Proverbs 14.31). If we could see the world through the eyes of God, we would look through a filter of compassion. God cares about our needs, our hurts, our brokenness. He understands our sinfulness – it does not shock or surprise God. But instead of judging us, God is ready to forgive, to heal, to restore us.

God is also a god of justice. In Isaiah God states that 'I, the LORD, love justice' (Isaiah 61.8). The Psalmist declares, 'The LORD works vindication and justice for all who are oppressed' (Psalm 103.6).

Jesus himself lived a life of compassion for 'the least'. He mended and cared for the sick, he forgave the sinful, he shared meals with prostitutes and tax collectors, and yet his compassion never undermined his sense of justice. Rather, he blended the two together. His love of God led him to grab a whip and throw out the merchants in the temple. When faced with injustice, Jesus fought against it with a holy passion.

God desires that we too 'Give justice to the weak and the orphan; maintain the right of the lowly and the destitute' (Psalm 82.3).

In the book of the prophet Micah, we read:

> He has told you, O mortal, what is good;
> and what does the LORD require of you
> but to do justice, and to love kindness,
> and to walk humbly with your God? (Micah 6.8)

Through the prophet, God tells us how to live, and in the person of Jesus Christ, God shows us how to live.

GROUP DISCUSSION

What are some factors that keep us from getting involved in social justice activities?

What is the Social Justice Tradition?

As we saw in the last section, Jesus distilled the law into two commandments: love God and love your neighbour. According to Luke's Gospel, a fellow Jew then asked Jesus, 'And who is my neighbour?'

Jesus answered by telling a story, or parable, about a person whom the Jews considered unclean, a Samaritan, who stops to help a man who has been robbed, stripped, beaten, and left beside the road to die. A Jewish priest and a Levite had seen the needy man but had passed by him without bothering to stop and help. The Samaritan treats and bandages the man's wounds, takes him to an inn, cares for him for a day, and then pays the innkeeper for his extended care. Jesus then asked the questioner, 'Which of these three, do you think, was a neighbour to the man?' and he responded, 'The one who showed him mercy.' Jesus said to him, 'Go and do likewise'. (Luke 10.29-37)

The Social Justice Tradition has been integral to the life of the Church. Throughout its history, men and women have dedicated their lives to caring for the hungry, the poor, the naked, the stranger, the sick, and the imprisoned. Think of the Salvation Army, Mother Teresa's Sisters of Mercy, World Vision and other relief efforts.

Often the compassionate response demands more than a shipment of food or medicine. There is an old proverb that says, 'Give a man a fish, and you have fed him for one day; teach him to fish, and you have fed him for a lifetime.' Bringing justice into a situation involves helping people learn skills so that they can support themselves.

Christ calls us to fight policies that discriminate on the basis of external appearances such as race and gender and social backgrounds such as class and religion; and to stand against societies and governments that oppress their people by denying them basic human rights. The Social Justice Stream has always called the Church to work for equity in all human relations and social structures. So must we if we truly love our neighbour.

Practising the Social Justice Tradition

One of the most remarkable aspects of practicing the Social Justice Tradition is its double effect: in the process of helping others, we, too, are helped. John Wesley once said that true happiness comes from helping others. We begin the task of 'carrying one another's burdens' out of compassion, but in the end we find that we too have been truly blessed.

There is, however, a pitfall we should be aware of before we enter into any project of service as part of practising the Social Justice Tradition. In his book *Celebration of Discipline*, Richard Foster notes the important difference between self-righteous service and true service. He lists nine important points to consider as we engage in works of compassion. These points could be read aloud by different members of the group.

1. Self-righteous service relies on human effort, whereas true service flows out of a relationship with God. Listen to the promptings of God as you begin and lean on his strength to do the task.
2. Self-righteous service is impressed with the 'big deal', whereas true service makes no distinction between the large and the small. Be indiscriminate in your choice, knowing that God often considers the small task the most important.
3. Self-righteous service requires external rewards, whereas true service rests contented in hiddenness. Avoid doing things for others as a means of getting applause or reward, relying instead on the divine nod of approval.
4. Self-righteous service is concerned with results, whereas true service is free of the need to calculate them. Do not let your expectations guide your service, and do not be disappointed if your service effects no external change.
5. Self-righteous service picks and chooses whom to serve, whereas true service is indiscriminate in its ministry. Be careful not to neglect the poor and the lowly in favour of the rich and powerful ... or vice versa!
6. Self-righteous service is affected by moods and whims, whereas true service ministers on the basis of need. Do not let your feelings, which

ebb and flow, determine your actions; rather let the service discipline your feelings.

7. Self-righteous service is temporary, whereas true service is ongoing. Compassion is a way of life which spontaneously meets human need, not merely an occasional helping hand.

8. Self-righteous service is insensitive, whereas true service withholds as freely as it gives. Listen with tenderness and patience before you begin. Be sensitive to what people really need, not merely what you think they need.

9. Self-righteous service fractures community, whereas true service builds community. Be careful not to let your 'good works' become debts that others must repay. Direct your efforts toward building unity in the community.

These guidelines are important for the following acts of service.

EXERCISES IN THE SOCIAL JUSTICE TRADITION

Each person should choose one of the following exercises and practise it before the next meeting. If possible, look at the exercises together before the end of this session.

The best way to start your task this week is to begin with this simple prayer: 'Lord Jesus, show me someone whom I can serve.'

1. Write a kind, encouraging letter.

This may seem like a small task, but it can work miracles. Take time to write a letter that tells someone how important he or she is to you. We seldom let people know how much they are appreciated. Or perhaps you know someone who is struggling with something – a decision, a failed marriage, a disappointment. Write a letter that tells him or her that you care and that you are available if they need to talk. 'Anxiety weighs down the human heart, but a good word cheers it up' (Proverbs 12.25).

2. Volunteer to help at a local charity or soup run.

Relief efforts and service organisations always need helping hands. Look in the telephone book or ask someone in your church for the name of a charity or soup run. Call and volunteer to help in any area. Such organisations usually need workers to stock shelves, serve food, clean storerooms, do clerical work, and undertake other such tasks. A few hours of your time will be greatly appreciated.

3. Guard the reputation of another person.

Although you cannot see it, a person's reputation is valuable, and you can guard and protect it by refusing to gossip or backbite. Paul urged Titus 'to speak evil of no one' (Titus 3.2a). By refusing to take part in discussions that focus on half-truths or faultfinding, you can contribute to the death of the rumour or criticism. If people you are talking with start to say gossipy or critical things of someone, smile and gently say, 'We don't know that's really true, do we?' or 'That doesn't sound like him (or her) at all.' Then simply change the subject. Your gentle demeanour and response can help others become aware of the harmful nature of their words.

4. Look for an injustice and address it.

If you open your eyes, you will begin to see areas in your home, workplace, community, or church that support injustice. First, examine yourself to make sure that you are not looking for a speck in your neighbour's eye and overlooking the two-by-four in your own (Matthew 7.3–5). In other words, ask yourself, 'Am I doing something that oppresses someone else?' Look for ways you might be taking advantage of someone, abusing that person's kindness, or stifling his or her growth. After a thorough self-examination you will be more able to look at the injustice you see around you.

You should always avoid advising people on the problem or condemning them for their actions, but if you are true to the task of addressing injustice, you will – at some point – need to voice your concern. For example, if someone in your workplace is doing something unethical (perhaps lying to customers about a product), you can bring the issue up with your colleague in a calm, tactful, and non-accusatory manner. Remember, the goal is not to hurt people, but to see justice reign.

5. Take a stand.

Is there racism, sexism, or some other form of discrimination in a club, a business, a community or an institution that you need to address? If so, discuss with the Spiritual Formation Group what your response should be. If your action involves some form of civil disobedience, engage in it peacefully, prayerfully, and compassionately. Be sure that the other members of the group support you with prayer and other appropriate actions.

Ending and beginning

We end with prayer for one another, and say the Lord's Prayer together, before deciding who will lead the next meeting.

SESSION SIX

Practising the Word-Centred Life

THE EVANGELICAL TRADITION

We open with silent prayer.

The footprints of God

GROUP DISCUSSION

How did everyone get on with the spiritual exercises undertaken during the week? What did people learn about God and about themselves?

Jesus and the Word-Centred Life

In the following two passages we see Jesus at the beginning of his ministry. Filled with the power of the Spirit, he goes to his home region, Galilee, and teaches in its synagogues.

Luke 4.16–19a; 42–44 to be read aloud.

> When he came to Nazareth, where he had been brought up, he went to the synagogue on the sabbath day, as was his custom. He stood up to read, and the scroll of the prophet Isaiah was given to him. He unrolled the scroll and found the place where it was written:
> 'The Spirit of the Lord is upon me,
> because he has anointed me to bring good news to the poor.
> He has sent me to proclaim release to the captives
> and recovery of sight to the blind,
> to let the oppressed go free,
> to proclaim the year of the Lord's favour.'

And he rolled up the scroll, gave it back to the attendant, and sat down. (Luke 4.16–19a)

At daybreak he departed and went into a deserted place. And the crowds were looking for him; and when they reached him, they wanted to prevent him from leaving them. But he said to them, 'I must proclaim the good news of the kingdom of God to the other cities also: for I was sent for this purpose.' So he continued proclaiming the message in the synagogues of Judea. (Luke 4.42–44)

GROUP DISCUSSION

How did you become aware of the good news of the kingdom of God? Did you hear it proclaimed by a person or did you read about it in the Bible?

Thinking it through

Residents of Galilee were considered backward by their fellow Jews, the cultured Judeans, for several reasons: Galilee was physically cut off from Judea by Samaria; much of its population lived in small towns; and its economy centred around agriculture and cottage industries. In fact, Galilee had been isolated from mainstream Jewish life for so long that its residents had distinct accents (Matthew 26.73).

But it is among the plain, ordinary, scorned folk of Galilee that Jesus begins his ministry. He comes to Nazareth and worships in the synagogue on the Sabbath. He proclaims the good news of the kingdom of God from the Scriptures to his former neighbours.

We must understand the shock Jesus' hearers feel when he points to himself as the fulfilment of the passage from Isaiah. For centuries they had hoped and waited for a Messiah who would free them from political oppression. Every Sabbath they had gone to their local synagogue where they sang Psalms, prayed for the Messiah to come, and listened to the Scriptures, depending upon their rabbi to interpret them. They had waited and waited. Numerous self-proclaimed Messiahs had lived . . . and died. Between Sabbaths many times their hope died when they were confronted by cruel soldiers or greedy tax collectors, but it came alive again when they listened to the promises of Scripture. Now here is the village carpenter, the son of Joseph and Mary, claiming to be the Messiah and proclaiming 'the year of the Lord's favour'. *Who does he think he is?*

They become enraged and try, but fail, to throw him over a cliff. Their reaction does not stop Jesus. He continues to proclaim the 'good news of the kingdom of God' throughout Galilee and in the synagogues of Judea, and even in Jerusalem, the centre of Judaism.

GROUP DISCUSSION

In order to appreciate the effect of Jesus' ministry, the following exercise can be done in the group, each person taking a brief time for imaginative reflection before sharing some of your reactions. Alternatively, it can be one of the suggested exercises for reflection at home before the next session.

Read John 7.1– 8. Imagine yourself as one of Jesus' brothers.

You have known Jesus since you were born; he is your older brother. You grew up in the same house and worked together in the carpentry shop. But he is acting crazy, going around the countryside healing people and preaching to crowds and making outlandish claims. Yet Jesus wants to keep out of the public eye. How do his actions make you feel? Do you feel ashamed? Proud? Angry? Jealous? Willing to side with his enemies? Do you share some of the same doubt Jesus' brothers did? If so, ask Jesus to help you overcome it.

God and the Word

God uses three central ways to reveal himself to us: the written word, the living Word, and the spoken word.

The written word

Most of us are familiar with the Bible, the word of God written.

The first section, the Hebrew law (or Torah), includes the Ten Commandments and was written first on tablets, then on rolled scrolls of parchment that were passed from generation to generation. Later the Hebrews added the 'Prophets' and the 'Writings'. God has used the Scriptures to communicate directly with his people for millennia. Like the early Hebrews, their descendants believe that the Scriptures are sacred and handle them with great care. They view them as God's actual words that were transcribed by ordinary human beings. Tradition tells us that when a Jewish scribe copies the books of the Scriptures, he washes his hands before he writes 'God'.

Christians call the Hebrew Scriptures the 'Old Testament' and, like their ancestors before them, view it as sacred, God's actual words transcribed by ordinary human beings.

In the 'New Testament', also sacred, we learn about Jesus, the beginnings of the Church, faithful Christian living, and our ultimate destiny in Revelation.

God has used the Scriptures to communicate directly with his people for millennia.

The living Word

Jesus Christ, the living Word, is God's clearest expression of himself. John 1.1 states, 'In the beginning was the Word (the Logos), and the Word was with God, and the Word was God.' As the Logos, Jesus reveals to us a God who creates, who loves, who heals, who understands, who blesses. God became one of us to show himself to us and to bring us back into his family. When we look into the face of Jesus, we see eyes that radiate compassion and lips that say 'God loves you'. We see God, because Jesus is God.

It is impossible to express fully the mystery of Jesus as the living Word. In Colossians, Paul tells us that Christ 'is the image of the invisible God, the firstborn of all creation; for in him all things in heaven and on earth were created, things visible and invisible . . . he himself is before all things, and in him all things hold together' (Colossians 1.15–16a; 17). We owe our very beings and our day-to-day welfare to Jesus Christ, the living Word. Thanksgiving can be our only response.

The spoken word

But it is the spoken word of God, the proclamation of the gospel, that is at the core of the Word-centred Life. The role of a word is to communicate. We speak the written word (the Bible) that tells about the living Word (Jesus Christ) so that hearers can establish a relationship with God.

'So faith comes from what is heard, and what is heard comes through the word of Christ' (Romans 10.17). Our task is not to proclaim our own words, but to proclaim God's Word to the nations.

GROUP DISCUSSION

Many of us learned that evangelism alone was at the heart of the Evangelical Tradition. Does the teaching that the Evangelical Tradition includes the written word, the living Word and the proclamation of the gospel help or hinder you?

What is the Evangelical Tradition?

In Romans, Paul asserts 'Everyone who calls on the name of the Lord shall be saved,' but then asks: 'But how are they to call on one in whom they have not believed? And how are they to believe in one of whom they have never heard? And how are they to hear without someone to proclaim him? And how are they to proclaim him unless they are sent? As it is written, "How beautiful are the feet of those who bring good news!"' (Romans 10.13–15).

By working backwards, we see the flow of the Evangelical Stream as well as its practice.

- First, a person must be 'sent' to those who have not heard the 'word'.

- Second, the messenger must proclaim it, or witness to it.

- Third, the listener must receive the word and believe.

- Fourth, the listener asks God to restore their relationship.

Jesus both proclaims and is the 'good news of the Kingdom of God'; he is the way back into God's love and care.

When the Pharisees asked Jesus when the kingdom would come, he responded, 'The kingdom of God is not coming with signs to be observed; nor will they say, "Look here it is!" Or "There it is!" For behold, the kingdom of God is in your midst' (Luke 17.21, NASB). And the kingdom in our midst – the life of God – is available to everyone who hears the gospel. This is the heart of the Evangelical Stream.

Practising the Evangelical Tradition

The three main aspects of The Evangelical Tradition – the Bible, Jesus Christ, and proclamation – are not easy to take on board. For a lot of people, the Bible is a very difficult book to read, much less understand. Others may not be ready to believe that Jesus Christ is the living Word, the Son of God, or feel that they need to have more faith. About proclaiming the gospel, many of us are often hesitant, fearing that we will offend someone or sound 'preachy'.

These are legitimate fears, but they should not prevent us from taking small steps so that our ability and faith gradually increase.

The following suggestions may help.

- A contemporary translation of the Bible is much easier to read than an older one such as the King James Version, where the English is nearly four hundred years old. A translation such as the New Revised Standard Version or a paraphrase/translation such as *The Message* can help many people when it comes to using the Bible regularly. Go to www.bibleresources.org.uk for help in selecting the Bible that is right for you.

- Keep in mind that we are reading the Bible with an ear to what God is saying to us, not simply studying it like a textbook. On one level we are trying to understand its message while on another level we are interacting with words that will mould our thoughts and our hearts. For this spiritual formation to take place, we should read the Bible slowly, repeating each verse several times, letting the words sink deep into our spirit.

- We ask Jesus Christ to increase our faith in him. James says that 'You do not have, because you do not ask' (James 4.2). Then, with the certainty that God will grant our request, we act. We read the Gospels over and over. We walk with Jesus down the dusty roads of Galilee, Judea, and Samaria. We listen to his teachings. And more. We get Jesus into us. And we claim the verse 'Faith is the assurance of things hoped for, the conviction of things not seen,' and trust that God will increase our belief (Hebrews 11.1).

- When sharing the gospel, we need to remember that we are to tell others what God has done, not to convert them. If we try to change people, we will end up frustrated and they, sensing our true motives, will be offended. By keeping the focus on what God has done to draw people back to him, and on what Jesus Christ is bringing into our lives, those we speak to will be hungry for what we have. We should always keep in mind that the Holy Spirit draws, not coerces, people into the kingdom of God.

EXERCISES IN
THE EVANGELICAL TRADITION

Each person should choose one of the following exercises and practise it
before the next meeting. Look at the exercises together before the end of
this session.

1. Memorise a verse of Scripture.

Select a verse unfamiliar to you from a favourite translation. You may
want to pick one of these excellent verses – Galatians 2.20; Romans 5.1;
John 3.16; Psalm 1.1; Ephesians 2.8 – or you may want to choose some
other verse. Memorising Scripture allows God's word to take root in your
thought life and in your inner heart. It is easier to memorise a verse one
phrase at a time rather than all at once. Keep adding phrases and saying
the verse to yourself throughout the day until you are able to repeat it
from memory.

2. Read one of the shorter books of the Bible out loud.

The Gospels, and even Paul's letters, were read aloud to the early
Christians in their gathered communities. Read one of Paul's shorter
letters out loud to yourself. Imagine how the Christians listening to those
words for the first time felt and responded.

3. Meditate on a brief passage about Jesus Christ.

Keep your selection simple: for example, John 1.1, John 1.14, Hebrews
1.1–2, or 1 John 1.1–3. Take twenty minutes or so to read the verse or
passage slowly and carefully. Pause after each sentence and reflect on it.
Ask questions: What does this sentence mean? What is God telling me
about himself? about Jesus Christ? about me? about others? If a particular
word or phrase stands out, spend additional time reflecting on it.

4. Imagine yourself as one of Jesus' brothers (see discussion earlier in this session).

Read John 7.1–8. You have known Jesus since you were born; he is your
older brother. You grew up in the same house and worked together in
the carpentry shop. But he is acting crazy, going around the countryside
healing people and preaching to crowds and making outlandish claims.
Yet Jesus wants to keep out of the public eye. How do his actions make
you feel? Do you feel ashamed? Proud? Angry? Jealous? Willing to side
with his enemies? Do you share some of the same doubt Jesus' brothers
did? If so, ask Jesus to help you overcome it.

5. Look for an opportunity to tell someone about your faith.

Prayer precedes these opportunities, so begin by praying that God will bring you into contact with someone who needs to hear about Jesus. Ask him to let you know in some way who is the right person and when is the right time. When that person asks how you are doing, or how things are going, you could begin speaking about the central place faith in Jesus Christ has in your life. Do not speak in a way that makes the person feel he or she is being judged or manipulated. Simply express what has happened to you and let that word go forth honestly.

6. Proclaim the gospel by your actions.

St. Francis reminds us, 'Always preach Christ; use words when necessary.' During the next few days let your actions speak for you, but before beginning, pray for the insight to see your life as others see it. Then, as you come into contact with people, pay particular attention to your actions and what they are conveying. The fruit of the Spirit (love, joy, peace, and so on) witnesses to the power of God. When people see these qualities in your life, they will instinctively want to know what makes you 'different'. By the end of this exercise you should be able to pick out areas in your life that speak well of Christ and the ones that need correcting.

Ending and beginning

We end with prayer for one another, and say the Lord's Prayer together, before deciding who will lead the next meeting.

SESSION SEVEN

Practising the Sacramental Life

THE INCARNATIONAL TRADITION

We open with silent prayer.

The footprints of God

GROUP DISCUSSION

How did everyone get on with the spiritual exercises undertaken during the week? What did people learn about God and about themselves?

Jesus and the Sacramental Life

In the following passage we confront the age-old division between work and faith. It was considered wrong in Jesus' day to 'work' on the Sabbath. Jesus makes an important distinction, which we will look at in more detail below.

Gospel Passage: Luke 13.10–17

Now he was teaching in one of the synagogues on the sabbath. And just then there appeared a woman with a spirit that had crippled her for eighteen years. She was bent over and was quite unable to stand up straight. When Jesus saw her, he called her over and said, 'Woman, you are set free from your ailment.' When he laid his hands on her, immediately she stood up straight and began praising God. But the leader of the synagogue, indignant because Jesus had cured on the sabbath, kept saying to the crowd, 'There are six days on which work ought to be done; come on those days and be cured, and not on the sabbath day.' But the Lord answered him and said, 'You hypocrites! Does not each of you on the sabbath untie his ox and his donkey from the manger, and lead it away to give it water? And ought not this woman, a daughter of Abraham whom Satan bound for eighteen long years, be set free from this bondage on the sabbath day?' When he said this, all his opponents were put to shame; and the entire crowd was rejoicing at all the wonderful things that he was doing.

GROUP DISCUSSION

The Sabbath has always been considered 'holy' in the Christian tradition, which has led to it being treated differently in some respects to weekdays. It is only recently, for example, that shops have been open on Sundays. Do you think it is important to keep Sunday special? How might you do this? Is it more difficult these days than perhaps it used to be?

Thinking it through

First-century synagogue services were similar to our present-day church services. The people sang songs (psalms), listened to the reading of Scripture, prayed, and heard a message, normally delivered by the local rabbi.

In this service Jesus is what we might call the guest speaker. Right in the middle of his talk a woman arrives, an unusual happening in itself. Most archaeologists believe that men worshipped on the ground floor of synagogues while women observed the service from the balcony. If this is true, then any woman who appeared among the men was not where she was supposed to be.

Jesus does what he was called to do – 'let the oppressed go free' (see Session Six, p.59) – and heals the woman. The leader then becomes furious and tries to regain control of his synagogue. He reminds worshippers that religious law is very clear that work should be done during the week, never on the Sabbath. To heal on the Sabbath is 'working'.

Jesus responds with an illustration everyone readily understands: all of you will work on the Sabbath to take your animals to water and keep them alive, but you won't lift a finger to help this woman! Are they worth more than she is?

We see no division between sacred and secular in the words and deeds of Jesus. While he observed the sacraments of his Jewish faith, he shattered the glass wall separating faith and work.

God and the Incarnation

The Trinity is at the heart of the Incarnational Tradition because Jesus Christ is The Incarnation. In the person of Jesus Christ, God became human, hence putting his blessing upon the material, physical world in which we live. God as Spirit created a physical body to inhabit; a marvellous, indescribable reality harmonising spirit and matter. By taking on all of the limitations of physical existence and living among us, God tells us that he loves matter. Because we are made of matter, what we say, what we do, and who we are, is invaluable.

God created humans as embodied spirits, and when he saw that we had lost our way, he became one of us to help us find our way back into his family.

By growing up in a family and taking part in everyday human activities like working, eating, laughing, washing, walking, weeping, talking, and more, Jesus put his stamp of approval on every aspect of human life. Nothing was exempt.

Likewise, Jesus affirmed our vocations by becoming an ordinary labourer – a carpenter – and a teacher – a rabbi.

In the Incarnation, God affirmed the value and goodness of human life and the goodness of the entire material world.

GROUP DISCUSSION

How much do you consider the everyday aspects of your life – cleaning house, loving your spouse, going to work – as important to God as the spiritual aspects?

What is the Incarnational Tradition?

As physical beings we find it easy to focus on the material, the things we can see and touch. We need food to live and we enjoy eating. Our bodies get cold so we buy clothes. Because we are sentient beings, everything we know about our world comes through our senses.

This presents a problem when we start exploring the world of the spirit. We can't smell, taste, touch, see, or hear the spiritual, so we hesitate to believe it is real. We relegate it to a special category and shove it into a 'pigeonhole', a box, allowing it to come out only on special 'holy' days or when we have a specific need such as physical healing.

The Holy Spirit helps us overcome this disunity by promoting the harmony of the physical and the spiritual. At their creation, Adam and Eve's bodies and spirits were in perfect harmony. But at the fall, their bodies took charge and started warring with their spirits. The Apostle Paul clearly describes this problem when he exclaims, 'For I do not do what I want, but I do the very thing that I hate' (Romans 7.15b).

The spiritual disciplines put us in a place where God can work his goodness into us and bring harmony into our lives. And when our bodies and our spirits start to come back into harmony, then we do away with the categories. We easily move between religious and everyday activities, treating them as being of equal value because God is present in both. And all that we say, all that we do, all that we are becomes a means to make God's presence real to those around us.

When we fast (whether it's from food, TV or anything else), we are telling our body that matters of the spirit are important. Serving another person for example puts his or her needs ahead of ours. In the discipline of simplicity we are freed from the tyranny of always getting our own way. The practice of worship reminds us that we are 'dust' (Psalm 103.14).

When our life is a 'seamless garment', we are free to reveal God to the world. We become wholly available to God, and he does his work through us. Our mind becomes the mind of God helping his children understand his love. Our hands become the hands of Jesus nursing the sick. Our voice becomes the voice of Christ proclaiming the good news of the kingdom of God. Our arms become the arms of the Holy Spirit loving the sinner unconditionally. As we let the power and life of God flow through us, we become the people he created us to be.

Practising the Incarnational Tradition

What steps can help us integrate our divided self?

The following suggestions can each be read by one or more members of the group and discussed briefly. They reflect the need for change on the inside, a prerequisite to changes on the outside in what we do and say.

1. We can try to cooperating with the Holy Spirit. All people put up barriers that exclude God even though they are his children. We might think of this as an invisible shield that takes the form of our skin, an

extra layer to keep God out. When we pray, 'God, I remove this barrier,' God responds and energises us.

2. We can actively think about life as a unit and in harmony rather than in terms of spirit/matter, sacred/secular, faith/work, soul/body, religious/worldly. Jesus showed us by his actions that life can be unified, that we can move readily in the power of God every day of the week, not just on 'holy' days.

3. We can think of our work as a 'calling', just as much as that of minister or priest. In the carpenter's shop Jesus served God when he served other people, making tables and chairs and cradles. We similarly serve God by whatever we do.

4. We can view the family or our group of friends as a place where God can be served rather than as a means to fulfil our own needs and wants. We can find God in the most menial of tasks.

5. We can stop thinking in terms of hierarchy or competition. A truly integrated person brings God, family and friends, and vocation together, spending time with each as needed rather than as dictated by any legalistic scheme. Since the CEO and the secretary are equally valuable, we respect and treat each person equally. All of our actions and activities are important in God's economy because we show forth the presence of God to the world.

We remember that our interior transformation takes time and occurs gradually. In conjunction with the other Traditions – Contemplative, Holiness, Charismatic, Social Justice, and Evangelical – the Incarnational Stream leads us deeper into the interior and guides our actions so that we can truly bring the presence of God to those closest to us and to our society. Through us the invisible world of the spirit becomes visible.

EXERCISES IN THE INCARNATIONAL TRADITION

As in each session, talk through the following exercises before deciding which each person will do between this and the next meeting.

1. Take an inventory of your life.

List on a piece of paper all of the activities that you are involved in such as work, church, clubs, housework, parenting, hobbies, sports. Be very specific. Now on a scale of 1 to 10 with 1 representing the least effective, decide how well you bring the presence of God into each activity. Don't be discouraged if the results are disappointing. Even though we may have been practising the disciplines for quite a while, change takes time. Pray, asking God to help you show forth his presence in those areas that have lower scores. Then, as you participate in the activities, imagine God working through you.

2. Remove the barrier that keeps God outside.

As you sit in a chair, imagine that you have an extra layer of skin or maybe a full 'body suit' that keeps God's Spirit out of the innermost parts of your being. Hold this in your mind for a moment. Then destroy or rip off the barrier and invite the Spirit of God to overwhelm you with his love, to take up permanent residence in your body, to make you a 'tabernacle'. Wait before God until you feel the work is complete, expressing your gratitude.

3. Do your work in honour of God.

In our culture we do things to honour famous people – awards, ceremonies, parades. Choose a day this week to do your work in honour of God. When you go to work, whatever form of transport you use, take it in a manner that brings respect to God. As you answer the telephone, or speak to someone, give the conversation and its results to God. While planting a tree, thank God for the beauty of his creation. Conduct the staff meeting, chat at the school gates, finish a piece of work, as if God is visibly present – an audience of One – observing everything that you do.

4. Begin to read a book by Dostoyevsky, Tolstoy, or Solzhenitsyn.

Fyodor Dostoyevsky, Leo Tolstoy, and Aleksandr Solzhenitsyn wove Christian faith into their literary works. Dostoyevsky writes about a Christ-figure, Prince Mishkin, in *The Idiot*. Tolstoy's *War and Peace* and *Anna Karenina* engage us in the great struggles of human souls. Solzhenitsyn integrates his faith into the warp and woof of *One Day in the Life of Ivan Denisovich* and *Cancer Ward*. You will probably need more than a week to read one of these books, although *One Day* is quite short and accessible.

5. Receive the sacrament of Communion, or the Eucharist.

On Sunday attend a church that will be serving Communion. Prepare to receive the sacrament by taking a mental inventory of ways God helped you bring his presence into your family, workplace, and social contacts during the previous few days. Then receive the Eucharist joyfully, and thankfully, knowing that Jesus Christ is truly present to you and longs to strengthen you and teach you daily.

Ending and beginning

We end with prayer for one another, and say the Lord's Prayer together, before deciding who will lead the next meeting.

Discovering a Practical Strategy for Spiritual Growth

THE SPIRITUAL FORMATION GROUP

We open with silent prayer.

The footprints of God

GROUP DISCUSSION

How did everyone get on with the spiritual exercises undertaken during the week? What did people learn about God and about themselves?

Jesus and our life together

Having completed the six sessions on the Traditions, we are nearly at the stage of doing our first 'trial' group in the pattern recommended for meeting on a regular basis.

In this section, we look at the suggested structure for the ongoing Spiritual Formation Group.

First, we remind ourselves of Christ's presence when we meet in his name.

Matthew 18.19–20 to be read aloud.

> 'Again, truly I tell you, if two of you agree on earth about anything you ask, it will be done for you by my Father in heaven. For where two or three are gathered in my name, I am there among them.'

Thinking it through

Far from leaving them on their own, Jesus promises his disciples that he will be with them forever. Christ is with us when we gather 'in his name'. He is the reason Christians come together. Jesus Christ called us to become disciples, so he must always be at the centre of our corporate gatherings.

If Jesus had simply died and left his followers to fend for themselves, Christian gatherings – whether large worship services or small-group fellowships – would be focused on the individuals who make up the groups. But quite the opposite is true: Christ has risen from the dead, and so our fellowships focus on him. It is very easy to focus on our needs, our failures, our efforts to 'get right' with God, but our worship must centre on Christ. It is Christ who calls us, Christ who empowers us, and Christ who unites us.

When we come together and agree on something, Christ assures us that God will do it. The word 'agree', however, means more than simply coming to a decision. The Greek word used here, 'symphoneo', implies a harmony that is achieved only through prayer and searching. Like a symphony, we are to practice and to pray and to work together until we are in tune. The unified voice we lift in prayer comes before the Father through the Son who has promised to answer our pleas.

When we gather in Jesus' name, we are not merely remembering Jesus because of what he said and did when he was on earth. We are actively encountering the living Christ because of what he has done and continues to do among us.

God and spiritual growth in his people

How do people grow in the spiritual life? As we have been exploring, one major way is to do spiritual exercises, or to practise the spiritual disciplines, within the framework of a Christian fellowship. How do the disciplines help us grow spiritually? The exercises create space in our lives where God can begin to transform us. Many times 'no trespassing' signs block God's entrance into the areas of our lives that need to be remoulded and reshaped. At other times we may think we are too busy to include God in our lives.

God has chosen spiritual exercises as the primary way to build our relationship with him. From the Bible we discover that the activities we have been learning about and doing – prayer, fasting, service, and so on – serve as instruction manuals that God uses to teach us how to live holy lives.

In looking at the Six Traditions, we have discovered spiritual disciplines which can help us live holy lives: these include prayer, studying the Bible, deeds of service, exercising the gifts of the Holy Spirit, working for justice and practising the presence of God.

Spiritual growth occurs when we focus on God and practise these disciplines. God loves us and wants to teach us, heal us, bless us, encourage us. He has chosen these and countless other exercises as a way to remove our 'No Trespassing' signs, to enter our lives, and to reshape them.

Earlier we noted that these exercises are best practised in fellowship with other Christians. There are three reasons for this.

- First, for our own sakes, God does not want us to isolate ourselves from each other and to grow further and further apart. He desires instead that we embrace each other, as sinners, and grow closer and closer together. The possibilities of sin will remain with us, no matter how far we travel in the Christian life. Also, by travelling together on the path of transformation, we help each other avoid the pitfall of the disciplines becoming deadly, self-righteous practices. We are fellow travellers, fellow sinners united in Christ's body.

- Second, God understands that we have more strength to do what is best for us when involved in a loving fellowship. Alone, we yield easily to apathy; together, we can resist the forces that attack us, including indifference. In Hebrews we read, 'And let us consider how we may spur one another on toward love and good works' (Hebrews 10:24).

- Third, God knows that we need guidance. From time to time we all need help in discerning what to do. Are we doing too much? Too little? Are we on the right path? Sometimes we cannot hear an answer because we are too close to a situation. Quite often we find our answer when simply listening to others as they share their experiences of failure and success.

GROUP DISCUSSION

Do you identify with the three needs listed below?

a. to grow closer to others

b. to be encouraged by others

c. to learn from others

How else might a Spiritual Formation Group help you grow spiritually?

Consolidating the Spiritual Formation Group

A few years ago a Princeton University poll revealed that the number-one priority for most Christians was 'personal spiritual growth'. In spite of this need, most churches do very little to meet it. Recognising our own need, we have been taking some small steps toward consistent spiritual growth and preparing to take larger steps. We have also been assembling many pieces. We will now fit those pieces together to form the Spiritual Formation Group mosaic.

First, we bring the strengths from the six traditions we have studied – Contemplative, Holiness, Charismatic, Social Justice, Evangelical, and Incarnational – into an intentional community – the Spiritual Formation Group. This balanced approach coupled with Christian fellowship helps us maintain equilibrium in our spiritual lives.

Second, we obtain material to help start the Spiritual Formation Group. This book provides the structure for starting a Spiritual Formation Group and a plan to continue meeting beyond the initial nine sessions. The end chapters of *Life Streams* contain ideas and exercises to give the direction we all need and answers the question that stymies many of us, What am I supposed to do? The ideas and exercises can also be used with the other resources on the spiritual life: *Celebration of Discipline*, *Devotional Classics*, and others (see Bibliography, p.105).

Third, the Spiritual Formation Group provides mutual encouragement and accountability. By joining forces, by 'synergising' energies, the group becomes greater than the sum of its individual members. Each person receives power and energy from the group as well as from the Lord to practise the spiritual disciplines.

GROUP DISCUSSION

Which of these three pieces do you need the most:

a. balance and community

b. structure, ideas, and exercises

c. encouragement and accountability

Working together as a Spiritual Formation Group

For the past several weeks we have been working together as a Spiritual Formation Group. At each meeting we individually chose an exercise, made a covenant with the group members to do the exercise before the next gathering, and then shared our experiences with each other. This is how a Spiritual Formation Group works together.

It is helpful to have such a structure. The suggested Order of Meeting (see p.79) is not designed to control or inhibit a group, but is in the form of an outline that will help a leader open, guide, and close the regular meeting.

The following few paragraphs are an introduction to the Order of Meeting, which is then given in full at the end of this guide. This will form the basis of each meeting once the group is under way properly. As we go through it please refer to each section in turn so that you become fully familiar with its structure.

As has been mentioned already, there is no single leader in a Spiritual Formation Group; everyone shares the leadership. To guide the group through the Order of Meeting is the leader's only responsibility. As we have said, it is a good idea to decide who will lead the next meeting at the close of each gathering.

It is suggested that each meeting is opened and closed in a similar way, giving the meeting focus and reminding people of the need for confidentiality.

Reference to the agreed covenant of the group gives the meeting purpose and running briefly through the spiritual disciplines brings to the fore what the group is working on.

A time for reading and reflection is included, with the choice of a reading from the Bible or from a suitable spiritual book being left to the group. This will be most fruitful if related to the questions that follow.

The 'Questions of The Heart' are the core of each meeting and the basis for discussion and mutual support. The questions are designed to help us share what God is doing in our lives. No one is expected to answer every question; everyone responds to those that apply to the exercises he or she did since the group's last meeting. People who see God working in their lives in another area may choose to answer one or more of the other questions.

The next section, entitled 'Looking Ahead', is when people choose an exercise that will help them move forward, and then share their intention with the rest of the group. We may want to give extra support to each other by recording each person's intent. This simple exercise is a powerful motivational tool; we become aware of what exercises others are doing, and they become aware of what exercises we are doing. In the process we experience guidance and encouragement. It is anyway a good idea to have a notebook or journal which can be used at home and in the group.

This planning time is crucial. We need to offer guidance, support, and be accountable to each other, and this can only be done when we make clear and definite plans and share them with each other. If we fail to plan, we plan to fail. The 'Ideas and Exercises' listed at the back of this book will provide lots of material for this section.

The next section that we earlier called 'Ending and Beginning' is the Lord's Prayer on the Order of Meeting. It focuses on supportive prayer for each other. We share needs and situations that would benefit from prayer. It is often helpful to write these concerns down so that we can remember to pray for them. Most groups then choose one or more members to pray for the concerns during a short time of intercessory prayer.

At the end, we pray the Lord's Prayer together.

SPIRITUAL FORMATION GROUP

Order of Meeting

The following is the formal Order of Meeting. It would be useful to have this as a separate document for reference, so that it can be used when the introductory sessions are complete. It is therefore set out in such a way here as to be photocopied as necessary or you can download it from the Renovaré website – www.renovare.info.

SPIRITUAL FORMATION GROUP

Order of Meeting

Opening words

After a few moments of silence, the leader for the week reads the following Opening Words aloud.

Welcome to the Spiritual Formation Group. May God's Holy Spirit bless us, and may we find fellowship and encouragement during this time together.

We gather together with one aim – to become better disciples of Jesus Christ. We do this by encouraging one another to keep Jesus' word, which, as he said, is what we naturally do when we love him (John 14.23–24). Through the grace of mutual accountability, we strive to inspire one another to love and good works.

Everything said here is in confidence and stays within these walls. Only then can we feel free to share honestly. This is how we help each other.

Covenant

As a group, read the Covenant aloud and in unison.

In utter dependence upon Jesus Christ as my ever-living Saviour, Teacher, Lord and Friend, I will seek continual renewal through spiritual exercises, spiritual gifts, and acts of service.

Common disciplines

Beginning with the leader, take turns reading the six Common Disciplines aloud:

By God's grace, I will set aside time regularly for prayer, meditation, and spiritual reading and will seek to practise the presence of God.

By God's grace, I will strive mightily against sin and will do deeds of love and mercy.

By God's grace, I will welcome the Holy Spirit, exercising the gifts and nurturing the fruit while living in the joy and power of the Spirit.

By God's grace, I will endeavour to serve others everywhere I can and will work for justice in all human relationships and social structures.

By God's grace, I will share my faith with others as God leads and will study the Scriptures regularly.

By God's grace, I will joyfully seek to show forth the presence of God in all that I am, in all that I do, in all that I say.

Reading and reflection

If you wish to include a suitable Bible passage then do so here. Relate this to the Questions of the Heart that follow. Alternatively include a short passage from a classic Christian spiritual book on the same themes, or simply move straight on to the next section.

Questions of the heart

Beginning with the leader, each member shares experiences from the previous week. The following may help focus the discussion. Answer at least the *first* question in each set.

In what ways has God made his presence known to you since our last meeting? What experiences of prayer, meditation and spiritual reading has God given you? What difficulties or frustrations have you encountered? What joys and delights?

What temptations have you faced since we met? How did you respond? Which disciplines has God used to lead you further into holiness of heart and life?

Have you sensed any influence or work of the Holy Spirit since we last met? What spiritual gifts has He enabled you to exercise? What was the outcome?

What fruit of the Spirit would you like to see increase in your life? Which disciplines might be useful in the effort?

What opportunities has God given you to serve others since our last meeting? How did you respond? Have you encountered any injustice to, or oppression of, others? Have you been able to work for justice or shalom?

Has God provided an opportunity for you to share your faith since we met? How did you respond? In what ways have you encountered Christ in your reading of the Scriptures? How has the Bible shaped the way you think and live?

In what ways have you been able to manifest the presence of God through your daily work since our last meeting? How has God fed and strengthened you through the ministry of word and sacrament?

Looking ahead

Beginning with the leader, allow time for each member to share his or her plans for the coming week. These questions may be used as guidelines. Writing these commitments down will help you remember what others are doing and give you a chance to pray for them.

On which area or areas would you like to work this week? What specific exercise or exercises would you like to try?

After each person has had a chance to share, the leader asks if anyone has a particular need or knows of situations that would benefit from prayer. Members can make notes of these so that they can pray for them during the week ahead. The leader also invites someone to lead the group in prayer for these concerns.

The Lord's Prayer

Finish by saying this (or another) version of the Lord's Prayer aloud, possibly joining hands.

Our Father, who art in heaven
hallowed be thy name.
Thy kingdom come,
thy will be done

on earth as it is in heaven.
Give us this day our daily bread,
and forgive us our trespasses
as we forgive those who trespass against us.
And lead us not into temptation
but deliver us from evil.
For thine is the kingdom, the power and the glory,
for ever and ever. Amen

Closing words

After the Lord's Prayer, the leader ends the meeting by reading the following Closing Words aloud and then asking for a volunteer to lead the next meeting.

Please remember that what we have heard here was spoken in confidence and should remain so. May the love, peace, and power of God be with us during this week.

READY TO FLY SOLO

Congratulations! We have gone through the Order of Meeting and know how a Spiritual Formation Group works. Now choose one exercise from Sessions Two to Seven that you have not done and determine to do it between now and the next meeting. Write down, perhaps on a photocopy of the Worksheet (see p.110), what you and the other members of the group are planning to do.

When we meet the next time, we will use the Order of Meeting as our guide. We have completed the Eight Beginning Sessions, and we are ready to have a regular meeting. Also, at the end of our next meeting we will turn to the extra section entitled Periodic Evaluation and use it to evaluate our group (what we liked, what we didn't like, what we would like to change, and so on). We will then decide if we want to continue meeting as a group and if we want to continue using this method. If we agree to continue gathering regularly, we will covenant to meet and to work together as a group for the next six months.

As usual, close with the words of the Lord's Prayer from the Order of Meeting.

May the ever-living Jesus Christ who is in our midst bless us and keep us until we meet again.

Evaluating the Group's Experience and Planning for the Future

Why evaluate?

In order for a small group to function effectively and continue to meet the needs of its members, it is crucial that the group periodically evaluate itself.

What does an evaluation do?

- **It restores vitality.**

  Small groups have a tendency to slip into routines that make their meetings seem mundane. By evaluating the group's dynamics, it is possible to restore its original vision and rekindle the members' initial enthusiasm.

- **It overcomes problems.**

  It is easy for a small group to develop relational or directional problems that slowly begin to undermine its effectiveness. By evaluating the way the group is working together to meet its goals, it is possible to repair some of these areas and to establish a more efficient structure.

- **It gives people a chance to share their needs and concerns.**

  A group's most common ailment is the unvoiced concern. When a group is no longer meeting our needs, we have a tendency to keep it to ourselves and simply stop attending. Later, when the other members learn that we have decided to quit, they are shocked and surprised. Evaluations help us share our current needs as well as offer us a graceful way to quit without hurting anyone's feelings.

When to evaluate

The following evaluation form should be used after a Spiritual Formation Group has held one introductory meeting, gone through the Eight Beginning Sessions in this workbook and held one regular meeting (a total of ten meetings including the first one).

Some groups centre one meeting around the evaluation; others do it at the conclusion of the regular meeting. However the evaluation is done, its use is important.

We recommend that a Spiritual Formation Group initially meets for a minimum of six months. This 'covenant period', or mutually agreed-upon time span, is long enough for the members to become acquainted with how a Spiritual Formation Group works and is short enough to keep it focused. A six-month covenant to work together, with the agreement that they will do an evaluation at its end, also allows members to fully experience mutual fellowship and encouragement before making a decision to meet for another six months.

Existing groups who have never done an evaluation should do one as soon as possible. This will help the members define the group and determine where it is going. While we recommend that new and existing groups do an evaluation every six months, it is certainly possible for them to do one at any time.

The following questionnaire contains questions that will help each member share his or her feelings about the group. It is important that everyone has a chance to speak; answering the questions one at a time will encourage members to respond. The person who volunteered to lead the meeting will guide the evaluation process.

If the evaluation is being done in a separate meeting, turn to the Order of Meeting (p.79) and follow the outline through the 'Opening Words' and the 'Covenant', then return to this point. If this is at the end of a regular meeting, begin here.

Spiritual Formation Group Evaluation Questionnaire

Allow each person a few moments to answer the questions if he or she wishes.

Personal questions (to be answered as each person wishes)

1. *Since one of my goals is 'to become an effective disciple of Jesus Christ', has this Spiritual Formation Group:*

   a. Increased my effectiveness substantially?

   b. Increased my effectiveness in small ways?

   c. Made no difference in my effectiveness?

2. *Do the same 'wheel' exercise that we did in Session One.* Below, the six Traditions are arranged around the spokes of a wheel. Using a scale of 1 to 10 (with 1 being the least proficient and closest to the centre of the wheel) estimate where you are in each area on the wheel spokes. Place dots at those points, then connect the dots from spoke to spoke to form a ring around the centre.

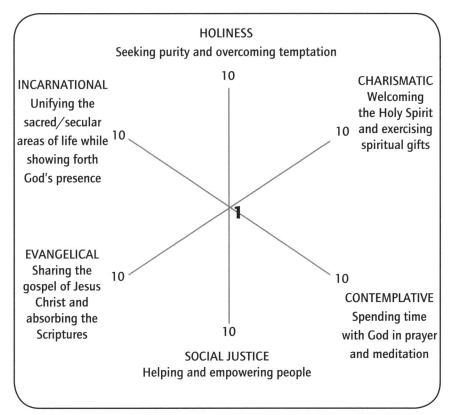

Now, compare this wheel to the one on page 28, then answer the following questions, circling the letters beside your choice. In which of the six Traditions have I seen the most growth?

   a. In the contemplative, or prayer-filled, life.

   b. In the holiness, or virtuous, life.

    c. In the charismatic, or Spirit-empowered, life.

    d. In the social justice, or compassionate, life.

    e. In the evangelical, or Word-centered, life.

    f. In the incarnational, or sacramental, life.

3. In which of the Six Traditions have I seen the least growth?

    a. In the contemplative, or prayer-filled, life.

    b. In the holiness, or virtuous, life.

    c. In the charismatic, or Spirit-empowered, life.

    d. In the social justice, or compassionate, life.

    e. In the evangelical, or Word-centered, life.

    f. In the incarnational, or sacramental, life.

The leader guides the discussion, keeping in mind that some members may hesitate to share their feelings about the Spiritual Formation Group. He or she reminds the members to be kind and honest, and takes notes of the suggestions and decisions made.

Group questions

1. Discuss each of the following areas by answering the question under each heading.

    a. *Direction*
    Are we moving towards our destination and reaching our goals, or are we wandering around with no real sense of direction?

    b. *Balance*
    Are our discussions equally balanced, allowing each member a chance to share, or do they sometimes get dominated by one or two of us?

    c. *Focus*
    Are our discussions focused, keeping on the topic, or do we get diverted by other concerns?

    d. *Teamwork*
    Are we working together as a team, supporting and encouraging one another to grow spiritually, or do we sometimes feel that each of us is training alone?

   e. *Environment*

   Are we creating an environment where we feel free to share what is in our hearts, not fearing how it will be received or wondering if it will be kept confidential, or is there a lack of trust that keeps us from sharing from the heart?

   f. *Attendance*

   Are all of us attending our meetings as faithfully as we can, or failing to attend regularly?

   g. *Hospitality*

   Are we willing to welcome new people into the group, or are we becoming a group where a new person feels uncomfortable or unwanted?

   h. *Time*

   Are we keeping within our time limits, or do our meetings last too long?

2. If you could keep only one thing about this group exactly like it is, what would it be?

3. If you could change only one thing about this group, what would it be?

   From what we have discussed,

   a. Should we continue as a group? If yes, how many months should we agree and commit to meet?

   b. Should we change anything about the group? If yes, what changes should we make?

Making a Covenant

If your group has decided to continue meeting, you may want to use the following to create a Covenant that specifically defines the terms and length of your commitment. You may want to have all of the members sign notes as another way to confirm your covenant.

- Who will lead the next meeting?

- When will we meet (time, day, frequency)?

- Where will we meet (location)?

- How long will the meeting last?

- What is our new Covenant period? When will we do the next evaluation (month)?

Ideas and Exercises

We all struggle to live the Traditions day by day. Discovering new activities that are rooted in the spiritual disciplines and the Traditions is a key part of our spiritual growth. Every time we need to incorporate one exercise into our weekly plans. The following exercises are divided into the six areas of discipleship that we have been studying and are only representative of the many different activities that help us go forward in the spiritual life. Since these ideas are simply suggestions that contain no laws or standards, feel free to modify them to fit your needs and situation.

Five cautions:

1. *Avoid vague goals.*

   SOLUTION: make your goals measurable (for example, read one chapter from the Bible each day).

2. *Don't try to do the impossible or unprofitable.*

   SOLUTION: be sure your plan is attainable. Ask your group 'Is this too much for me to try?'

3. *Don't distance yourself from the exercises.*

   SOLUTION: personalise the activities by doing them frequently and trying new ones often.

4. *Refrain from procrastination.*

   SOLUTION: make specific plans now (for example, meet God in prayer every morning at 7:30).

5. *In spite of Cautions 1 and 4, avoid becoming rigid or legalistic.*

   SOLUTION: be flexible when planning by focusing on the interior practice, not the exterior activity.

Remember: 'When we fail to plan, we plan to fail.'

Practising the Prayer-Filled Life: The Contemplative Tradition

1. Pray for ten minutes each morning or evening.

2. Pray without words (in silence) for five minutes a day.

3. Pray a short prayer throughout the day, for example, the hesychastic prayer 'Lord Jesus Christ, have mercy on me, a sinner' or the verse 'Create in me a clean heart, O God, and put a new and right spirit within me' (Psalm 51.10).

4. Set aside an hour that will be free of distraction. Use the time for solitude, prayer, and meditation on the Bible.

5. Read a section from a devotional classic, such as Augustine's *Confessions*, Brother Lawrence's *The Practice of the Presence of God* or Madame Guyon's *Experiencing the Depths of Jesus Christ.*

6. Write out a prayer in your journal. You may wish to keep it private, or you may wish to share it with your group. Write the letter as if it were addressed to God, telling him how you feel.

7. Learn to appreciate God through his creation. Take a walk in a park or simply sit and watch a sunset. Consider the majesty of the world, giving thanks and praise for all of God's creation.

8. Set aside fifteen minutes for a time of thanksgiving. Thank God for everything you can think of. Do not worry about intercession or confession; this is a time simply to give thanks.

9. Practise the art of listening to God. Meditate on a verse of Scripture, being attentive to what God wants to tell you. Note the words in the verse. Does anything stand out? Turn the verse into a prayer. Ask God to teach you during this time of silence.

10. Hold people and situations before God in prayer. Take ten minutes a day to bring your friends and loved ones before God. Do not worry about words; simply imagine Jesus standing beside them before the throne of grace. Let God minister to all of their cares and hurts.

11. Pray for the leaders in your church. Find a time this week to pray specifically for your pastors and other leaders. Ask God to give them strength and wisdom and compassion. Pray for their protection.

12. Try 'arrow prayers.' When you see someone – anyone – silently pray for that person. Travelling on a bus, standing in a queue, sitting in a room – wherever you are, inwardly ask the Lord to give those around you joy, to touch their lives with his presence.

13. See if you can wake up praying. Give your day to God, asking him to guide you through each meeting, each conversation, each appointment.

14. Take a 'prayer walk' this week. Choose crowded urban streets where you can bless many with prayer, or go to a park or woods where you can rediscover that the earth and everything in it are the Lord's.

15. Pray as you walk, jog, swim or do any other form of exercise. Try blessing the homes you pass. Thank God for your friends who play sport or walk the dog with you. Even try praying for your tennis opponent!

16. Make a note of other ideas that help you to practise the prayer-filled life and add these to the list.

Other ideas

1. _____

_____

2. _____

_____

3. _____

_____

4, _____

_____

5. _____

_____

6. _____

_____

7. _____

_____

8. _____

Practising the Virtuous Life: The Holiness Tradition

1. Work on taming your tongue; speak only when necessary.

2. Try a twenty-four-hour fast to discipline your appetite. Eat no food from one lunch to another, skipping dinner and breakfast. Modify the fast by drinking fruit juice and plenty of water. Use the time you save by not eating to read your Bible.

3. Resolve to overcome temptation with silence and prayer. Instead of fighting or running from temptation, stand in silence, praying for God to give you strength.

4. Fast from the television for a week. Many find television programmes addictive, and they are certainly time-consuming. By not watching television for a week, you will be able to discern its effect upon your life. Again, use the time you gain to try some other spiritual discipline or simply to enjoy your family, perhaps playing a game or taking a walk together.

5. Be a 'gossip-buster'. Whenever you or someone you are with begin to gossip, quickly end it. Guide the conversation to a different subject.

6. Practise the art of speaking positively. Resolve to make two positive remarks about someone or something for every negative remark you make. Be careful not to get too far in debt!

7. Spend ten minutes each morning thinking about good things. Discipline your thoughts until they readily focus on the true, the honourable, the just, the pure, the pleasing, the commendable (Philippians 4.8).

8. Memorise the Ten Commandments (Exodus 20). These laws were 'sweeter than honey' to the psalmist (Psalm 19.10). Memorise them as a way to make them a more conscious part of your daily life.

9. Write out a confession in your journal. One of the best ways to get back 'on track' is to confess the things you have done or left undone. Be honest. God knows your faults and failings – you won't be telling him anything he does not already know! The exercise is for your benefit, not God's.

10. Cultivate integrity in your speech by focusing on simplicity and honesty in all that you say. Watch for guile and deception, which can creep into your speech in subtle ways. Be ruthless as you seek to tell the truth in everything.

11. Do a 'covet' check in your life. Are you enviously desiring anything? The Tenth Commandment tells us to not covet our neighbour's possessions.

Unchecked, covetousness leads to constant turmoil. Make a 'wish list' of all the things you would like to have and then destroy the list while asking God to help you let go of your desire to possess. Finally, offer a prayer of thanksgiving for all that you have.

12. Do a 'treasure' check in your life. Are there things that you prize too much? Jesus warned us not to place our hope in things that will decay and perish. The rich young ruler (Luke 18.18–30) kept all the commandments but lacked one thing: the ability to let go of his wealth. If you cannot freely give a treasure away, maybe it possesses you more than you possess it. Give it away and experience the freedom that comes when you relinquish a treasure.

13. Keep the Sabbath. 'Remember the Sabbath day and keep it holy' is one of the most neglected of the Ten Commandments (Exodus 20.8). The Sabbath is actually God's gift to a frazzled world. Sit down with your family and discuss how you can set aside one day (usually Sunday) for rest and recreation. Refuse to do any work, even the catch-up housework that presses you. Resist the guilt and simply rest in God. Allow yourself permission to do nothing, absolutely nothing.

14. Set aside an hour for 'holy leisure'. Find an hour when you can nap on a couch, or lie in a hammock, or relax over a coffee. God, who made us, realises we need rest and will bless our 'holy leisure'.

15. Read *The Pursuit of Holiness*. This bestseller by Jerry Bridges reveals the undiluted truth about sin, temptation, and the unparalleled freedoms that come from saying 'no'.

16. Make a note of other ideas that help you practise the virtuous life and add these to the list.

Other ideas

1. _____

_____

2. _____

_____

3. _____

_____

4. _____

Practising the Spirit-Empowered Life: The Charismatic Tradition

1. Search the Scriptures to discover your spiritual gifts. Romans 12.6–8 and 1 Corinthians 12.8–11 list gifts that we are to strive for and exercise as members of the body of Christ. Read the passages, pray about them, and seek understanding. You may want to ask someone you respect to recommend a book on the subject and then read it. Explore the 'spirit-empowered' roles. Ephesians 4.11–13 lists several leadership positions in the Church. Read the passage, asking the Spirit to direct your search as to how you can best serve the body of Christ.

2. Pray for the Holy Spirit. Jesus said that we must 'ask' for the Holy Spirit (Luke 11.13). Do you feel that the Spirit is present and active in your life? If not, spend an hour this week in prayer, asking the Lord for the Holy Spirit's real and life-giving presence.

3. Spend time reading about the 'fruit' of the Spirit. Galatians 5.22 lists the fruit or 'virtues' of the Spirit. The presence of that fruit is a sure sign God's Spirit is working in your life. Choose one fruit that you would like to see increase in your life, pray for its increase, and seek ways you can nurture its growth.

4. Bless others with your 'fruit' What fruit of the Spirit is most evident in your life (Galatians 5.22)? This week consciously be a conduit for the love, joy, peace, patience, kindness, generosity, faithfulness, gentleness, and self-control that the Spirit has given you.

5. Allow the Holy Spirit to become part of your prayer life. When you are praying this week, ask the Spirit to intercede when you cannot find words to express your concerns and your joys.

6. Welcome the illuminating work of the Spirit. One of the Spirit's functions is to make the words of the Bible come to life. When reading the Scriptures this week, open your mind to this 'Divine Interpreter'.

7. Put on your armour. As Christians, we are given divine equipment called the 'Armour of God' (Ephesians 6.10–17). List the different pieces of armour and ask the Spirit which one you need most at this time. When the answer comes, ask the Spirit to add this piece to your array of virtues so that you can withstand the devil's attacks.

8. Exercise your spiritual gifts. If you have discovered your spiritual gifts (see exercise 1 above), spend an hour this week exercising them in your local church.

9. Seek others' counsel about how you can best use your spiritual gifts. The Spirit sometimes gives guidance through other people. Ask a few friends whom you trust and who know you well what they see as your spiritual gifts and how they see those gifts best used. From this exercise you may reach a new awareness concerning your service in the body of Christ.

10. Really worship when you go to church this week. Walk through the door with 'a spirit of thanksgiving'. Sit in silence prior to the service. Meditate on God's mercy and majesty. Sing the hymns with enthusiasm. Fill the sanctuary with prayer. Above all, praise God. You may find this practice infects the people sitting around you with joy and thanksgiving.

11. Study the Scripture passages about the Holy Spirit. Use a concordance or a chain-reference Bible to find verses that refer to the Holy Spirit – his nature, role, and deeds. Highlight those references that you find new and exciting.

12. Pray for the Spirit to give you confidence in the promises of God in Christ. Begin by reading Romans 8. The Holy Spirit is able to verify your position as a child of God the Father. Let the Spirit teach you how to pray to God as his child, saying 'Abba, Father', and give you a life of confidence before God.

13. Read Tony Campolo's book *How to Be Pentecostal Without Speaking in Tongues*. It is an excellent introduction to the charismatic life, focusing on the 'vital aliveness' found in charismatic communities while avoiding the excesses found in every Tradition.

14. For fifteen minutes a day this week, wait on the Holy Spirit. Allow the Spirit to come into every corner of your life – your secrets, your desires, your failings, your victories, your all.

15. Make a note of other ideas that help you practise the spirit-empowered life and add these to the list.

Other ideas

1. _____

_____

2. _____

_____

3. _____

Practising the Compassionate Life: The Social Justice Tradition

1. Write a supportive letter this week to someone you feel may be needing a word of encouragement.

2. If you live with others, help out around the house. This may seem minor, but household chores are usually done grudgingly. Your willingness to do more than your share of work will be a real service to the others in the household.

3. Spend an afternoon working at a project for the homeless or marginalised. Your help is sorely needed, even if you can only sweep floors.

4. Donate blood. We are giving the gift of life when we give blood. Call your local blood bank and make an appointment.

5. Recycle your rubbish. Caring for the environment is an issue of social justice. Recycling what you throw away increases the next generation's chance for a bright future.

6. Help a friend in need. Do you know someone who needs assistance? If so, help that person. The job may be hanging wallpaper, grocery shopping, helping with a move or fixing the roof. Volunteering to help is a simple way to care for your neighbour.

7. Write to your Member of Parliament, local Councillor or representative and share your views. Is there an issue you feel strongly about? Be sure you have the facts straight and are expressing genuine Christian concern, not just prejudice.

8. Join a prison ministry. Your local church should know about groups that regularly minister to prisoners (and their families) in your area. Contact such a group and go with them to visit the inmates, who often feel forgotten in their isolation. Jesus told us that when we visit them, we are visiting him (Matthew 25.31–46).

9. Address an injustice with compassion. Is someone being treated unfairly? Do not be silent when your words could make a difference.

10. Practise the service of hiddenness. Do a kind deed (for example, sweeping a drive or calling on nursing home residents) without being asked or expecting recognition.

11. Serve others with your words. Protect people's reputations and speak well of others as a way of serving them. Kind words are great deeds.

12. Serve others by letting them have 'space'. We sometimes overwhelm people or consume their time or usurp their freedom with our expectations. Make a concerted effort to give people space. Ask them what they want to do or if they want to be alone or if they are free to talk before imposing your expectations upon them.

13. Serve others by letting others serve you. Are you guilty of not letting other people do things for you? Hold a door? Buy a cup of coffee? Make a photocopy? It is a gift to others to let them serve you; do not deny them this joy.

14. Read a book that discusses social justice issues. *The Politics of Jesus* by John Howard Yoder will force you to ask hard questions. You may also want to read Donald Kraybill's book, *The Upside-Down Kingdom*. Though you may not agree with everything these authors say, they should stimulate your thinking.

15. Write a one-page response this week to the following question: What is the most pressing social justice issue today, and what position should I, as a Christian, take? Share the paper with the other members of your Spiritual Formation Group.

16. Make a note of other ideas that help you practise the compassionate life and add these to the list.

Other ideas

1. _____

_____

2. _____

_____

3. _____

_____

4. _____

_____

5. _____

_____

Practising the Word-Centred Life: The Evangelical Tradition

1. Read the Bible for fifteen minutes a day. Choose a method of reading (for example, a chapter or a section a day) and follow it. Let the Bible influence the course of each day.

2. Meditate on John 1.1. Write the verse on 3x5 cards and put them (1) on your bathroom mirror, (2) on the dashboard of your car, or (3) near the place where you spend a lot of time. As often as possible, pause, read the verse, and meditate on the mystery of Jesus Christ as the living Word of God.

3. Ponder John the Baptist's role. Read John 1.6–9 several times, paying particular attention to what John was to Jesus (a witness), and what his task was (to testify about Jesus). Consider how John's example can help you be more assertive in your proclamation of the gospel.

4. Read a chapter of the Bible before falling asleep. Reading from the Bible just before we retire for the night is a nice way to end the day. It also helps us awake with the Word of God on our minds. You may want to read the chapter aloud with your children or your spouse or your college flatmate.

5. As you carry out your regular activities this week, think about the following question: How has my new-found understanding of Jesus as the living Word of God affected the practice of my faith? Record your response.

6. Talk about your faith in Jesus Christ with a relative or close friend. Often we neglect to talk about our faith with our friends and family, the most important people in our lives.

7. Meditate on a psalm once a day. The psalms are wonderful prayers that help us commune with God. Let the words of the psalms be your words. Read them slowly, over and over, until they become your prayers.

8. Meditate on the mystery of God entering history. Read John 1.14, remembering that 'Word' in this verse refers to Jesus Christ. The apostle John writes that 'the Word became flesh.' Hold this mystery before God and ask him to let it take root in the deepest recesses of your soul.

9. Make a real effort to reach others with the message of Christ. When you are talking with someone, guide the conversation into the issues that affect your life deeply such as life, death, meaning, and so on. Ask the person how he or she feels. If you discern little interest, politely drop

the subject. But if you sense a yearning to hear more, freely share what Christ means to you.

10. Memorise a verse or passage of Scripture. Some people like to memorise 'theme' verses (for example, verses that relate to God's power). Choose a verse (or even two or three) and recite it to your Spiritual Formation Group during the next meeting.

11. Describe the 'living Word' in your own words. First read the description of Jesus' eternal and physical life that is recorded in 1 John 1.1–3 several times. Then put the same thoughts into your own words, writing them in your journal.

12. Get acquainted with one of your neighbours. Simple friendliness can often afford opportunities to share God's goodness.

13. Study the Bible. Use a Bible that has study notes or get a good commentary and delve deeply into a passage, a chapter, or an entire book.

14. Read Revelation 1.12–20. When John saw the living Christ, he fell at his feet as though dead. How do you respond to Christ's presence? With fear? Dread? Confusion? Awe? Gratitude? Thank God for sending Jesus Christ to be our ever living Saviour, Teacher, Lord, and Friend. If you experience fear or dread or confusion about Christ's role, ask God to replace those feelings with love.

15. Rediscover the gospel of Jesus Christ. Read Peter's sermon on the day of Pentecost in Acts 2.14–36 and answer these questions, writing them on a piece of paper: Who was Jesus? What did he do? What is the proof? What were the results? Now write down how those answers should affect your life.

16. Make a note of other ideas that help you practise the word-centred life and add these to the list.

Other ideas

1. _____

_____

2. _____

_____

3. _____

Practising the Sacramental Life: The Incarnational Tradition

1. Choose a day this week to do everything in honour of God. Drive your car, answer the telephone, conduct the staff meeting, greet people, and enter data in the computer to the audience of One.

2. Receive the sacrament of Communion or Eucharist. Attend a church that will be serving Communion. Receive Eucharist joyfully, knowing that Jesus Christ is truly present to you and longs to strengthen and teach you daily.

3. Read *One Day in the Life of Ivan Denisovich*. Aleksandr Solzhenitsyn integrates his faith into the warp and woof of *One Day*, following in the tradition of novelists Fyodor Dostoyevsky and Leo Tolstoy.

4. Remove the barrier that keeps God outside. Imagine that you are wearing full body armour that keeps God's spirit out of the innermost parts of your being. Remove it, invite God in, and wait until you feel the work is complete, giving thanks at the end.

5. Help your church organise an art show. Artists – painters, potters, photographers, sculptors, weavers, and others – creatively express the imago Dei, the image of God, through their art. Some of the greatest artists ever were Christian. Organise an art show of the work done by members of your fellowship.

6. Read *The Journal and Major Essays of John Woolman*. Woolman was an eighteenth-century tailor, businessman, and minister of Christ whose tender conscience and persuasive manner awakened the hard hearts of Colonial Americans to the evils of slavery. Woolman's life is a stellar example of how the Incarnational Tradition works.

7. Attend services at a synagogue on the Sabbath. It is difficult to understand many of the stories in the Gospels unless we become familiar with the Jewish faith. Pay special attention to the liturgical aspects of the service.

8. Attend a Christian church outside your tradition. If you belong to a liturgical church (Catholic, Anglican, Lutheran), attend a 'free church' on a Sunday . . . and vice versa. Participate as fully as possible, feeling and absorbing the presence of God in the songs, prayers, sermon or homily, and sacraments.

9. Bring the presence of God to the ill. Contact a nursing home and make arrangements to visit the patients. As you converse with someone, perhaps in the communal lounge, place your hand on his or her arm

or hand, open yourself to God, and ask him to fill that person with his presence.

10. Listen to Handel's *Messiah*. This glorious oratorio has endured for over two hundred years and broken down the sacred/secular walls in the world of music. Listen to a recording of the complete work, paying particular attention to the words that flowed out of George Frideric Handel's faith.

11. Ask God to help you solve problems. Bring God into your workplace by doing this. Formality is not required: quick, silent prayers spoken before or during a telephone conversation or a meeting are heard by God too.

12. Bless your home. If you have not already done so, walk through your house and bless the rooms. Most of us spend the majority of our lives in our homes and fail to invite God into them.

13. Spend time with children. If children live in your neighbourhood, make a special effort to engage them in conversation. Young children are so transparent that they help us see God.

14. Take God with you wherever you go. During the next few days make a special effort to be a 'tabernacle' where God dwells. Co-operate with God to bring good wherever you walk – in the park, in your home, in your church – by praying for those you meet.

15. Invite God to your meals. For one week, make a special effort to sense the presence of the risen Lord during your mealtimes with other people. It is important to open a meal with prayer, although any prayer during the meal should be silent unless special prayer concerns are voiced.

16. Make a note of other ideas that help you practise the sacramental life and add these to the list.

Other ideas

1.

2.

3.

4. _____

_____

5. _____

_____

6. _____

_____

7. _____

_____

8. _____

_____

9. _____

_____

Bibliography

These are a few of the most significant books related to Renované and lyfe. Visit your local Christian or High Street bookshop or search on the web for the latest publishers and stockists.

Renované Resource Catalogue

Foster, Richard J. **Celebration of Discipline**. Richard Foster's original and most popular book. Offers critical insights into how to practise twelve Spiritual Disciplines: meditation, prayer, fasting, study, simplicity, solitude, submission, service, confession, worship, guidance, and celebration. Published by Hodder & Stoughton, paperback and unabridged CD.

Foster, Richard J. **Freedom of Simplicity** (21st Century Edition). Explains the complexity of simplicity, looks at its biblical roots, and discusses its practice in personal, family, church, and world arenas. Published by Hodder & Stoughton, paperback.

Foster, Richard J. **Money, Sex and Power: The Challenge of the Disciplined Life**. Explores three great ethical themes – money, sex and power – and helps people of faith trying to live faithfully determine their proper place. Published by Hodder & Stoughton, paperback.

Foster, Richard J. **Prayer: Finding the Heart's True Home**. Warm, compelling, and sensitive primer which helps us understand, experience, and practise prayer in its many forms – from simple to unceasing prayer, from sacramental to petitionary prayer. Published by Hodder & Stoughton, paperback and unabridged CD (Harper Audio).

Foster, Richard J. **Seeking the Kingdom**. Features key passages from Foster's books (*Celebration of Discipline, Freedom of Simplicity, The Challenge of the Disciplined Life* and *Prayer*) that are tied to a key biblical passage and reflection. Published by Hodder & Stoughton, paperback.

Foster, Richard J. **Streams of Living Water**. A spiritual history of the Church that explores Six Traditions of Christian faith and life, examines the contribution of each, and seeks a balanced path to spiritual renewal by combining the best from each Tradition or stream. Publisher various, paperback and abridged CD/audiotape (Hovel Audio).

Foster, Richard J., Beebe, Gayle, Graybeal, Lynda L., Oden, Thomas C. & Willard, Dallas (eds) **The Renovaré Spiritual Formation Bible**. Now published as The Life with God Bible (see below).

Foster, Richard J. & Griffin, Emilie (eds) **Spiritual Classics**. Selected excerpts drawn from the heritage of nearly 2,000 years of Christian writing. Based on the Spiritual Disciplines, each reading ends with Scripture, reflection questions, exercises, and a meditation. Published by HarperOne, paperback.

Foster, Richard J. & Smith, James Bryan **Devotional Classics** (revised edition). Fifty-two readings from classic Christian devotional writers that are accompanied by a meditation, linked Bible passage, questions, and exercises. Published by HarperCollins, paperback.

Foster, Richard J. with Willard, Dallas, Brueggemann, Walter, Peterson, Eugene H. **The Life with God Bible** NRSV. Previously published as The Renovaré Spiritual Formation Bible. Published by HarperCollins, paperback.

Foster, Richard J. with Willard, Dallas, Carney, Glandion, Campbell, Margaret, Skramstad, George & Stewart, Jim (eds) **Celebration of Discipline Video Curriculum**. 13-session group resource that includes Leader's Guide, 2 Participant's Guides, DVD with 13 presentations, and CD-Rom containing script and other resources. An excellent small group resource for studying Celebration of Discipline and Richard Foster's thinking and writing. Published by LifeSprings.

Smith, James Bryan **The Good and Beautiful God** and **The Good and Beautiful Life**. Part of a series called The Apprentice, these books have been called 'the best practice I have seen in Christian spiritual formation' by Dallas Willard. Published by Hodder & Stoughton, paperback.

Smith, James Bryan **A Little Handbook of God's Love**. Smith distils basic principles of Christian love and provides a new paradigm for relationship with God, self, and others that is based on acceptance and care. Published by Hodder & Stoughton, paperback.

Willard, Dallas **The Divine Conspiracy**. This masterpiece explores what it means to live in God's kingdom here and now as a disciple of Jesus Christ rather than waiting solely for the hereafter. As he describes apprenticeship to Jesus, Willard brings a fresh perspective to the Sermon on the Mount. Published by HarperCollins, paperback and unabridged CD.

Willard, Dallas **The Great Omission**. Considers the Great Omission of the Church, the failure not only to preach the gospel but also to show people how to embody and live out the good news; to make not only Christians but disciples of Jesus Christ. Published by Monarch Books, paperback.

Willard, Dallas **Hearing God**. Originally titled In Search of Guidance, this enlivening guide is rich in spiritual insight that helps Christians create an intimate partnership with God and become co-labourers with him in the kingdom. Published by InterVarsity Press, paperback and audio CD (Hovel Audio).

Willard, Dallas **Renovation of the Heart.** Explains the why and how of Christian spiritual formation and discusses the God-ordained process that 'brings every element of our being' – heart, mind, soul, strength – 'working from the inside out, into harmony with the will of God.' Published by InterVarsity Press, paperback and unabridged audio book.

Willard, Dallas **The Spirit of the Disciplines.** Establishes the theological foundation for the classic *Disciplines of the Spirit,* discusses how they transform us into Christlikeness, and explains that discipleship for the Christian is not an option, but a requirement. Published by Hodder & Stoughton, paperback and audio CD (Hovel Audio).

Willard, Dallas with Crabb, Larry & Ortberg, John. **Renovation of the Heart Video Curriculum**. Group resource that includes one copy of *Renovation of the Heart*, Leader's Guide, two Participant's Guides, DVD with thirteen presentations, and CD-Rom containing script and other resources. An excellent small group resource for studying *Renovation of the Heart* and Dallas Willard's thinking and writing. Published by LifeSprings.

Willard, Dallas with Johnson, Jan **Hearing God through the Year**. Being close to God means communicating with him – telling him what is on our hearts in prayer and understanding what he is saying to us. The second part of this conversation is so important – and so difficult. How do we hear God? The readings in this devotional will help answer that question. Published by InterVarsity Press, paperback.

Willard, Dallas with Simpson, Don **Revolution of Character**. In this more accessible version of *Renovation of the Heart*, Willard explores five critical elements that have an impact on us: heart, mind, body, social life, and soul. Publisher InterVarsity Press. Paperback.

Lyfe Resource Catalogue

Casey, Michael **Sacred Reading**. Published by HarperCollins and Ligouri/Triumph, paperback.

Fee, Gordon & Stuart, Douglas **How to Read the Bible for all its Worth**. Published by Zondervan, paperback.

Peace, Richard **Contemplative Bible Reading**. Published by Navpress, paperback.

Spriggs, David **Connected Christianity**. Published by BRF, paperback.

Sproul, R.C. **Knowing Scripture** (revised edition). Published by InterVarsity Press, paperback.

Wright, Tom **New Testament Guides for Everyone**. Published by SPCK, Westminster John Knox Press, paperback.

The Bible Speaks Today series. Published by InterVarsity Press, paperback.

Crossway Bible Guides. Published by InterVarsity Press, paperback.

The Drama of Scripture. Published by SPCK, Erdmans, paperback.

The Interpretation of the Bible in Church. Published by Pontifical Biblical Commission.

The Lion Handbook to the Bible. Published by Lion Hudson, paperback.

New Bible Dictionary. Published by InterVarsity Press, paperback.

The Street Bible. Published by Zondervan, hardcover.

CD/DVDs

CDs/DVDs are also available from Christian bookshops or from online stockists.

Gospel of John (DVD). Be there – as Jesus turns water into wine and raises Lazarus from death. A British and Canadian cast bring the complete Gospel of John to life in this powerful new dramatisation by award-winning director Philip Saville.

Images of Salvation (CD-Rom). This educational CD-Rom combines an extensive treasury of 180 medieval images on key Christian themes, together with transparently clear explanations of the biblical, doctrinal and art historical context.

The Miracle Maker (DVD). It's a story that's been told for 2000 years – but never like this! The Miracle Maker combines lifelike 3D model animation with graphically striking 2D animation in this brilliant new portrayal of the life of Jesus, told through the eyes of a child.

Run in Motion (DVD). A unique DVD resource with a wealth of innovative short items designed to explore a range of life issues, using personal stories, Bible narratives, dramas and images.

Testament (DVD). Nine of the Old Testament tales are retold, using illustrations which draw on the great religious works of art, the latest innovations in computer and puppet technology, and the imaginations of the world's leading animators.

Worksheet

MY MEASURABLE, ATTAINABLE, PERSONAL, SPECIFIC PLAN

I plan to do the exercise(s) listed below _____ times between now and our next meeting. (You do not have to choose an exercise from all of the areas.)

Contemplative _____

_____

Holiness _____

_____

Charismatic _____

_____

Social Justice _____

_____

Evangelical _____

_____

Incarnational _____

_____

Date _____ Signed _____

This page may be photocopied for personal use.

Other members' plans

Name _____   _____

_____

_____

Name _____   _____

_____

_____

Name _____   _____

_____

_____

Name _____   _____

_____

_____

'Cast all your anxiety on [God], because he cares for you.' (1 Pet. 5.7)

Prayer concerns: _____

_____

_____

Other notes: _____

_____

_____